PORTRAITS AND DOCUMENTS

THE LATER
MIDDLE AGES
1216–1485

PORTRAITS AND DOCUMENTS

A SERIES OF HISTORICAL SOURCE BOOKS

GENERAL EDITOR: J. S. MILLWARD

The Early Middle Ages edited by Derek Baker
871–1216

The Later Middle Ages edited by Derek Baker
1216–1485

The Sixteenth Century edited by J. S. Millward
1485–1603

The Seventeenth Century edited by J. S. Millward
1603–1714

The Eighteenth Century edited by J. S. Millward and
H. P. Arnold–Craft
1714–1783

The Earlier Nineteenth Century edited by Dennis Holman
1783–1867

The Later Nineteenth Century edited by Peter Teed
and Michael Clark
(in preparation)

The Twentieth Century edited by Michael Clark
and Peter Teed
(in preparation)

PORTRAITS AND DOCUMENTS

THE LATER MIDDLE AGES
1216—1485

Edited by

DEREK BAKER

*Lecturer in History
at the University of Edinburgh*

HUTCHINSON EDUCATIONAL

HUTCHINSON EDUCATIONAL LTD
178–202 Great Portland Street, London W1

London Melbourne Sydney
Auckland Bombay Toronto
Johannesburg New York

First published 1968

*This book has been set in Fournier, printed in Great Britain
on Smooth Wove paper by Anchor Press, and
bound by Wm. Brendon, both of Tiptree, Essex*

09 086790 4 (cased)
09 086791 2 (paperback)

Contents

38501

2 THE CHURCH

3 LAND AND PEOPLE

Illustrations

Acknowledgements

Acknowledgement is gladly made to the following for permission to use copyright material:

Cambridge University Press for extracts from *Social Life in Britain from the Conquest to the Reformation* and *Life in the Middle Ages*, both edited by G. G. Coulton, *Readings in English Social History* edited by R. B. Morgan, *The Religious Orders in England* by David Knowles and *The English Church in the Fourteenth Century* by W. A. Pantin; the Folio Society for extracts from *The History of King Richard III* edited by P. Kendall and *The Hundred Years War* edited by P. E. Thompson; Harper and Row for extracts from *Sources of English Constitutional History* by C. Stephenson and F. G. Marcham; Manchester University Press for extracts from *The Anonimalle Chronicle* edited by V. H. Galbraith and *Chapters in Medieval Administrative History* by T. F. Tout; Thomas Nelson for extracts from *The Life of Edward II* edited by N. Denholm-Young; the Clarendon Press for extracts from *Henry III and the Lord Edward* by F. M. Powicke; Penguin Books Ltd for extracts from *The Canterbury Tales* edited by N. Coghill, *Piers the Ploughman* edited by J. F. Goodridge and *Historical Interpretation* by J. J. Bagley; University of Pennsylvania for an extract from *Custumals of Battle Abbey* translated by D. C. Munro; J. M. Dent for extracts from *The Paston Letters* edited by J. Fenn (Everyman Library); Secker and Warburg for extracts from *The Wars of the Roses* by J. R. Lander.

Every effort has been made to trace the owners of copyright material. The editor apologises for any omissions, and would be grateful to know of them so that acknowledgement may be made in any future editions.

Preface

In this volume, as in its predecessor, I have tried to keep both footnotes and editorial comment to a minimum, the only real problem occurring with documents written in the emerging literary English of the period. With most of these I have used modern versions, but one or two I have left in the original, to instance the spelling and form of the language. With these some notes have been necessary, but by and large they are intelligible with a little effort, and should be interesting to read.

My thanks are particularly due to John Millward, John Stevens and Susan Phillpott for their patience, kindness and help during the production of this book—a process which at times must have seemed as confused and interminable as the later Middle Ages themselves. Such mistakes as exist are, of course, mine.

DEREK BAKER

Introduction

Material for the history of the later mediaeval period is at once more abundant and more limited than for the earlier period. The elaboration of government, at all levels, in both Church and State is reflected in the mass of official documents available to the historian, but there is less personal, intimate observation to supplement this wealth of material; and where individual comment is encountered it seems all too often harsh, cynical and bitter. This situation, however, reflects the age itself. Government and administration may be becoming increasingly complex and sophisticated, but in this period five kings lose their thrones and their lives, and judicial murder becomes a commonplace. Chivalry and courtly love may be in vogue, but such ideals seem unrelated to the incidents of foreign and domestic wars, or the conduct of men like Gaveston or Thomas of Lancaster. The Papacy may possess wide authority and an elaborate machinery of government, and have found in the mendicants a new form and renewed fervour in regular life, but there is increasingly vocal criticism of papal exactions and schisms, and the decline of the mendicants is perhaps more remarkable than their initial impact. The age, in fact, is one of ferment, of growth and decay, ideal and disillusion intermixed, and it is important to see it as such: not merely as a period of decline and decadence arbitrarily terminated at the end of the fifteenth century by new monarchy and new learning. Parliament has its roots in the stability of English local government and society; lollardry embodies an intellectual inquisitiveness and a militant desire for reform besides much else, and if Margery Kempe seems thoroughly mediaeval in her attitudes and postures, in the intensity of her personal experience, and in her expression and description of it, she is difficult, as a laywoman, to fit into any accepted mediaeval category. The latest historian of the fifteenth century comments that 'so far from running down in this period, religion, not merely in literary and artistic forms, but in the fervour of corporate devotion and in popular appeal, achieves a place in the ordinary life of the country which it has seldom been accorded by historians of pre-Reformation England'[1], and this judgement may be applied to the whole of the achievement of later mediaeval England.

DEREK BAKER

1. E. F. Jacob, *The Fifteenth Century* (1961), p. 686.

KING AND GOVERNMENT

❖❖

Henry III

Source: Matthew Paris, *English History*, trans. J. A. Giles (1852–4) Vol. III pp. 382–3

This king Henry commenced the rebuilding of the church of Westminster, but did not complete it. In proportion as the king was considered to be deficient in prudence in worldly actions, so he was more distinguished for his devotion to the Lord; for it was his custom every day to hear three sung masses, and as he wished to hear more he assiduously assisted at the celebration of private masses, and when the priest elevated the body of our Lord he usually held the hand of the priest, and kissed it . . .

King Henry was of middling stature, and compact in body. The eyelid of one eye hung down so as to hide some part of the eyeball. He possessed robust strength, and was inconsiderate in his acts, but as they generally came to fortunate and happy results many thought that he was designated by the prophet Merlin, when speaking of the lynx, as penetrating everything with his eye.

❖

Henry III : Policies and Opposition

Source: Matthew Paris *op. cit.,* Vol. I pp. 67–8

[1237] King Henry III trusting to evil advice, contrary to what was his duty or expedient for him, estranged himself from the counsels of his natural subjects, and became stiff-necked against his well-wishers and those who looked to the advantage of the kingdom, and managed its affairs but little or not at all according to their advice. In order to have some cunning pretexts for extorting money from them, he declared on his oath, at a conference to which he had called the nobles from a distance that he was entirely destitute of money and in a state of the greatest need; he therefore most urgently begged of them to grant him the thirtieth part of property throughout the kingdom, that the dignity of him, the king, and that of the kingdom might be supported in a more honourable manner, and be established on a firmer foundation. The nobles were greatly troubled at hearing this, and replied that they were so often oppressed in this way, and saw so many foreigners fattening on their property, that the kingdom was weakened by poverty, and that manifold dangers were impending over it. However, after much discussion, inasmuch as the king humbled himself and promised that he would thenceforth abide by their counsels without hesitation, the thirtieth part of all moveable property was granted to him, though not without great difficulty. This he afterwards ordered to be collected and estimated, not at the royal valuation but according to the common value, and not to be placed in convents and castles, as had been pre-arranged and determined on, nor to be expended at the discretion of the nobles, but, without taking the advice of any one of the natural subjects of his kingdom, he gave it to foreigners to be carried abroad, and he became like a man bewitched, as if he had no sense. A murmur therefore arose amongst the people, and the indignation of the nobles waxed hot.

Richard, Earl of Cornwall, the king's brother was the first to call the king to account, and reproached him sharply for the great desolation caused by him in the kingdom. . . . Still, however, the king rejected his advice, as well as that of his other natural subjects, and grew worse and worse in the madness he had conceived . . . By these and similar ravings the king now drew blood from the hearts of his nobles, and he also had as counsellors infamous and mistrusted men, who were said to forment these deeds of his, and who, consequently, were exceedingly hateful to the English nobles, although they derived their origin from the same kingdom; and these were John, Earl of Lincoln, Simon [de Montfort], Earl of Leicester, and Geoffrey, a brother of the Temple.

✦

The Quarrel between Henry III and de Montfort (1252)

Source: Matthew Paris, *op. cit.*, Vol. II pp. 487–8

[1252] When the earl [Simon de Montfort] had given sufficient proofs of his innocence, and the adverse party had been refuted and silenced, the king still spoke against him, but when he perceived that Earl Richard and all the rest were in favour of Earl Simon, as they were ruled by prudence, he did not dare, although provoked to do so, to put the royal severity in force against him. Still, by thoughtless speeches they provoked the anger each of the other, and rashly recalled to mind things which had passed long since. The earl for instance, stated how he had rescued the king at Saintonges from the snares of the French; how, when he was on the point of starting for Gascony for the first time, the king had advised him to crush the traitors, how he had given him his charter for holding the guardianship of the country for six years; and how he had promised to afford him effectual aid and counsel, which had not been fulfilled,

3

And, he added, 'My lord king, your words should be stable and trustworthy. Keep your agreement with me, or keep your promise to me, in accordance with the tenor of your charter, or repay me the money which I have expended in your service, for it is well-known that I have irreparably impoverished my earldom for the sake of your honour.' To this the king hastily and ill-advisedly replied 'Be well assured that I will not observe the compact, in regard to any of my promises, with you, an unworthy traitor, who would, if you could, be the supplanter of your sovereign. For it is allowed one to break his compact when the others break theirs, and to deal so without shame with those who are so shameless.' The earl on hearing these words was highly incensed, and rising, he loudly declared that the king had lied in this speech, 'And,' said he, 'were it not that he is sheltered by his kingly name and dignity, it would have been a bad hour in which he gave utterance to such a speech.' At this the king, who could scarcely contain himself for rage, would have ordered him to be seized on the spot, had he not been well-assured that such a proceeding would not on any account have been allowed by the nobles.

A Foreign Favourite (1252)

Source: Matthew Paris, *op. cit.*, Vol. II p. 522

The king [Henry III], however, persisted in his usual extravagances, and as if in revenge for this opposition of the prelates, continued to distribute the vacant escheats and revenues amongst unknown, scurrilous, and undeserving foreigners, in order to inflict an irreparable wound upon the heads of his natural subjects. Not to mention others, we think it right to mention in this volume the following case, as one out of many. In the service of Geoffrey de Lusignan, the king's brother, was a certain chaplain, who served as a fool and buffoon to the king, the said Geoffrey his master, and all the court, and whose sayings, like those of a silly jester and club-bearer, contributed to their amusement, and excited their laughter; and on this man the king bestowed the rich church of Preston, which had formerly belonged to William Haverhull, the lately-deceased treasurer of the king, the yearly proceeds of which church amounted to more than a hundred pounds. This same chaplain, a Poitevin by birth, utterly ignorant alike in manners and learning, we have seen pelting the king, his brother Geoffrey, and other nobles, whilst walking in the orchard of St Albans, with turf, stones, and green apples, and pressing the juice of unripe grapes in their eyes, like one devoid of sense. Despicable alike in his gesture, mode of speech, and habits, as well as in size and personal appearance, this man might be considered a stage actor rather than a priest as he was, to the great disgrace of the priestly order. Such are the persons to whom the King of England intrusts the care and guardianship of many thousands of souls, rejecting such a vast number of learned, prudent, and proper men as England has given birth to, who know the language of the natives, and how to instruct the ignorant.

✧

The Baronial Crisis (1258–1266)

Sources: 1 Letter of Henry III
          2 The Provisions of Oxford (1258)
          3 The Provisions of Westminster (1259)
          4 The Decision of Louis IX (1264)
Select Charters, ed. W. Stubbs (1913), pp. 372–96, trans. C. Stephenson and F. G. Marcham, *Sources of English Constitutional History* (1937), p. 142

1. LETTER OF HENRY III

The king to all . . . You are to know that, through an oath given on our behalf by Robert Waleran, we have granted to the nobles and magnates of our kingdom that, by twelve faithful men of our council already elected and by twelve other faithful men of ours elected on the part of those nobles, who are to convene at Oxford one month after the feast of Pentecost next, the state of our kingdom shall be ordered, rectified, and reformed according to what they shall think best to enact for the honour of God and our faith and the good of our kingdom. And if, perchance, any of those elected on our part are absent, those who are present shall be permitted to substitute others in place of the absentees; and the same shall be done [with regard to those elected] on the part of the aforesaid nobles and faithful men of ours. And whatever is ordained in this matter by the twenty-four elected by both sides and sworn to the undertaking, or by the majority of them, we will inviolably observe, wishing and henceforth straitly enjoining that their ordinance be inviolably observed by all. And whatever security those men, or the majority of them, may provide for the observance of this matter, we will fully grant and cause to be granted. We also attest that Edward, our first-born son, through an oath personally taken, has by his letters granted that he will faithfully and inviolably observe, and will cause ever to be observed, all that has been expressed and granted above, so far as in him lies. Furthermore, the said earls and barons have promised that, on the completion of the business noted above, they will strive in good faith to see that a common aid is rendered to us by the community of our kingdom. . . . Given at Westminster, May 2.

2. THE PROVISIONS OF OXFORD (1258)

It has been provided that from each county there shall be elected four discreet and lawful knights who, on every day that the county [court] is held, shall assemble to hear all complaints touching any wrongs and injuries inflicted on any persons by sheriffs, bailiffs, or any other men, and to make the attachments that pertain to the said complaints [for keeping] until the first arrival of the chief justiciar in those parts: so that they shall take from the plaintiff adequate pledges for his prosecution [of the case], and from the defendant for his coming and standing trial before the said justiciar on his first arrival; and that the four knights aforesaid shall have all the said complaints enrolled, together with their attachments, in proper order and sequence—namely, for each hundred separately and by itself—so that the said justiciar, on his first arrival, can hear and settle the aforesaid complaints singly from each hundred. And they shall inform the sheriff that they are summoning all his hundredmen and bailiffs before the said justiciar on his next arrival, for a day and a place which he will make known to them: so that every hundred-man shall cause all plaintiffs and defendants of his bailiwick to come in succession, according to what the aforesaid justiciar shall bring to trial from the aforesaid hundred; also as many men and such men—both knights and other free and lawful men—as may be required for best proving the truth of the matter. [This, however, is to be done] in such a way that all are not troubled at one and the same time; rather let [only] as many come as can be [used in cases to be] tried and concluded in one day.

Likewise it is provided that no knight of the aforesaid counties, by virtue of an assurance that he is not to be placed on juries or assizes, shall be excused by a charter of the lord king or be exempt from [the obligations of] this provision thus made for the common good of the whole kingdom.

Elected on the part of the lord king: the lord bishop of London; the lord bishop of Winchester; the lord [Henry], son of the king of Germany; the lord John, earl de Warenne; the lord Guy de Lusignan; the lord William de Valence; the lord John, earl of Warwick; the lord John Mansel; Brother John of Darlington; the abbot of Westminster; the lord Henry of Hengham.

Elected on the part of the earls and barons: the lord bishop of Worcester; the lord Simon, earl of Leicester; the lord Richard, earl of Gloucester; the lord Humphrey, earl of Hereford; the lord Roger Marshal; the lord Roger de Mortimer; the lord John Fitz-Geoffrey; the lord Hugh le Bigot; the lord Richard de Gray; the lord William Bardulf; the lord Peter de Montfort; the lord Hugh le Despenser. And if it should happen that of necessity any one of these can not be present, the rest of them shall elect whom they please in place of the absentee, namely, another person needful for carrying on that business. . . .

The twelve on the king's side have chosen from the twelve on the side of the community the earl Roger Marshal and Hugh le Bigot. And the party of the community has chosen from the twelve who are on the side of the king the earl of Warwick and John Mansel. And these four have power to elect the council of the king; and when they have made the election, they shall designate those [elected] to the twenty-four. And that shall hold on which the majority of these [four] agree. . . .

Concerning the state of Holy Church—It should be remembered that the state of Holy Church is to be amended by the twenty-four chosen to reform the state of the kingdom of England—at what time and place they think best, according to the powers that they hold by writ of the king of England.

Concerning the chief justice—[It has been decided] furthermore that a chief justice—or two [chief justices]—shall be appointed; also what power he shall have; and that he shall be [in office] for only one year, so that at the end of the year he shall render account of his term before the king and the royal council and before the man who is to follow him [in office].

Concerning the treasurer and the exchequer—The same [has been decided] with regard to the treasurer; so that he shall render account at the end of the year. And according to the ordinance of the said twenty-four, other good men are to be appointed to the exchequer, whither all the issues of the land are to come, and not elsewhere. And let that be amended which seems in need of amendment.

Concerning the chancellor—The same [has been decided] with regard to the chancellor; so that he shall render account of his term at the end of the year, and that merely by the king's will he shall seal nothing out of course, but shall do so by [the advice of] the council that surrounds the king.

Concerning the power of the justice and of the bailiffs: The chief justice has power to redress the misdeeds of all other justices, of bailiffs, of earls, of barons, and of all other people, according to the rightful law of the land. And writs are to be pleaded according to

8

the law of the land in the proper places. And [it has been decided] that the justices shall accept nothing unless it is a present of bread and wine and like things: namely, such meat and drink as have been customarily brought for the day to the tables of the chief men. And this same regulation shall be understood [to hold] for all the king's councillors and all his bailiffs. And [it has been ordered] that no bailiff, by virtue of his office or of some plea, shall take any fee, either by his own hand or in any manner through another person. And if he is convicted [of so doing], let him be punished: likewise the man who gives [the fee]. And the king, if it is suitable, shall give [fees] to his justices and to his people who serve him, so that they shall have no need of taking anything from others.

Concerning the sheriffs: As sheriffs there shall be appointed loyal persons, good men who are landholders; so that in each county there shall be as sheriff a feudal tenant of the same county, who shall well, loyally, and justly treat the people of the county. And [it is ordered] that he shall take no fee; that he shall be sheriff for no more than a year in all; that during the year he shall render his accounts at the exchequer and be responsible for his term [of office]; that the king, from the royal income, shall make [allowance] to him in proportion to his receipts, so that he may rightly keep the county; and that he shall take no fees, neither he nor his bailiffs. And if they are convicted [of such wrongdoing], let them be punished. It should be remembered that, with regard to the Jewry and the wardens of the Jewry, such reforms are to be established as shall carry out the oath in this respect.

Concerning the escheators: Good escheators are to be appointed. And [it is ordered] that they shall take nothing from goods of deceased persons whose lands ought to be in the king's hands; but that, if a debt is owing to him, the escheators shall have free administration of the goods until they have carried out the king's wishes—and this according to the provision in the charter of liberties. Also [it is ordered] that inquiry shall be made concerning the misdeeds committed there by escheators, and that redress shall be made for such [wrongs]. Nor shall tallage or anything else be taken, except as it should be according to the charter of liberties. The charter of liberties is to be strictly observed.

Concerning the exchange of London: It should be remembered to establish reforms touching the exchange of London; also touching the city of London and all the other cities of the king, which have been brought to shame and ruin by tallages and other oppressions.

Concerning the household of the king and queen: It should be remembered to reform the household of the king and queen.

Concerning the parliaments, as to how many shall be held annually and in what manner: It should be remembered that the twenty-four have ordained that there are to be three parliaments in a year: the first on the octave of St Michael, the second on the morrow of Candlemas, and the third on the first day of June, that is to say, three weeks before [the feast of] St John. To these three parliaments the chosen councillors of the king shall come, even if they are not summoned, in order to examine the state of the kingdom and to consider the common needs of the kingdom, and likewise of the king; and by the king's command [they shall come] also at other times, whenever it is necessary. So too it should be remembered that the community is to elect twelve good men, who shall come to the three parliaments and at other times, when there is need and when the king and his council summon them to consider the affairs of the king and the kingdom. And [it has been decided] that the community shall hold as established whatever these twelve shall do—and this is to reduce the cost to the community. Fifteen are to be named by these four men—that is to say, by the earl Marshal, the earl of Warwick, Hugh le Bigot, and John Mansel—who have been elected by the twenty-four to name the aforesaid fifteen, who are to form the king's council. And they are to be confirmed by the aforesaid twenty-four, or by the majority of those men. And they shall have the power of advising the king in good faith concerning the government of the kingdom and concerning all matters that pertain to the king or kingdom; and if amending and redressing everything that they shall consider in need of amendment or redress. And [they shall have authority] over the chief justice and over all other people. And if they cannot all be present, that shall be firm and establishd which the majority of them shall enact. . . .

In the year 1259 from the Incarnation of the Lord, the forty-third of the reign of King Henry, son of King John, at a meeting of the lord king and his magnates at Westminster on Michaelmas fortnight, the provisions hereinunder written by the common counsel and consent of the said king and his magnates, were enacted and published by the same king and his magnates in this form:

1. With regard to the performance of suit to the courts of the magnates and of other lords who have such courts, it is provided and established by general agreement that no one who is enfeoffed by charter shall henceforth be distrained to perform suit to his lord's court, unless he is specifically obliged by the tenor of his charter to perform the suit; with the sole exception of those whose ancestors were accustomed to perform suit of this kind, or who themselves [were accustomed so to do], before the first crossing of the said lord king into Brittany—after the time of which crossing twenty-nine and a half years had elapsed down to the time that this constitution was made. And likewise no one enfeoffed without charter since the time of the Conquest, or by other ancient enfeoffment, shall be distrained to perform suit of this king, unless he or his ancestors were accustomed to perform it before the first crossing of the lord king into Brittany. . . .

4. With regard to the sheriff's tourn, it is provided that, unless their presence is specially demanded, archbishops, bishops, abbots, priors, earls, and barons, or other men of religion, or women, shall not of necessity come thither. . . . And the tourns shall be held according to the form of the king's Great Charter, and as they were customarily held in the time of the kings John and Richard.

5. It is also provided that neither on the eyres of the justices nor in the [courts of the] counties nor in the courts of barons shall fines henceforth be taken from anybody for miskenning, or for avoidance of trouble on that score. . . .

8. Moreover, with regard to charters of exemption and liberty, [to the effect] that those securing them are not to be put on assizes, juries, or recognitions, it is provided that, if their oath is so essential that without it justice cannot be administered . . . they shall be

forced to swear, saving to them their aforesaid liberty and exemption in other respects. . . .

11. Henceforth no one except the lord king and his ministers shall be permitted for any cause whatsoever, to levy distraints outside his fief, or on a royal or common highway. . . .

16. Hereafter no one but the king shall hold in his court a plea concerning false judgment rendered in a court of his tenant; for pleas of this sort especially pertain to the crown and dignity of the king. . . .

18. Without the king's writ, no one may henceforth distrain his free tenants to respond concerning their free tenements or anything that pertains to their free tenements. Nor may he cause his free tenants against their will to take oaths; so that no one may do this without the king's precept. . . .

21. Hereafter itinerant justices shall not amerce vills on their eyres because particular twelve-year-old persons do not come before sheriffs and coroners for inquests concerning a man's death or other matters pertaining to the crown; so long as, nevertheless, enough men come from those vills for satisfactorily carrying out such inquests.

22. No judgment of murder shall henceforth be rendered before the justices in a case that is adjudged merely one of accident; but [a judgment of] murder shall be proper in the case of a man feloniously slain and not otherwise. . . .

4. THE DECISION OF LOUIS IX (1264)

In the name of the Father and the Son and the Holy Spirit. By our [present] decision or ordinance we quash and annul all the aforesaid provisions, ordinances, statutes, and obligations, however called [The Provisions of Oxford], and whatever has followed from them or by occasion of them, especially since it appears that the supreme pontiff by his letters has proclaimed them quashed and annulled; ordaining that as well the said king as all the barons and other who have consented to the present arbitration, and who in any way have bound themselves to observe the aforesaid [provisions], shall be utterly quit and absolved of the same. We likewise add that, by virtue of force of the aforesaid provisions or obligations or ordinances, or of any authority already granted by the king on that account, no one shall make new statutes or hold or observe those already made; nor ought any one, through non-observance of the aforesaid [provisions], to be held the enemy, either principal or otherwise, of any one else, of for that reason incur any penalty. . . . We also decree and ordain that the aforesaid king at his own volition may freely appoint, dismiss, and remove the chief justice, chancellor, treasurer, counsellors, lesser justices, sheriffs, and any other officials and ministers of his kingdom and his household, as he was used and able to do before the time of the provisions aforesaid. Furthermore, we repeal and quash the statute made to the effect that the kingdom of England should henceforth be governed by natives and that all aliens should leave the kingdom, never to return, except those whose residence the faithful men of the kingdom commonly agreed to, ordaining by our decision that aliens may safely remain in the said kingdom, and that the king may safely call to his counsel such aliens and natives as shall seem to him useful and loyal, just as he was able to do before the time aforesaid. Likewise we declare and ordain that the said king shall have full power and unrestricted rule within his kingdom and its appurtenances, and shall in all things and in every way enjoy such status and such full power as he enjoyed before the time aforesaid. By the present ordinance, however, we do not wish or intend in any way to derogate from royal privileges, charters, liberties, establishments, and praiseworthy customs of the kingdom of England existing before the time of the same provisions. . . .

Now this our ordinance or decision we have promulgated at Amiens on the morrow of the blessed Vincent the Martyr, A.D. 1263, in the month of January. In testimony whereof we have caused our seal to be attached to the present letters.

Simon de Montfort

Source: Matthew Paris, *op. cit.,* Vol. III p. 355

Thus ended the labours of that noble man Earl Simon, who gave up not only his property, but also his person, to defend the poor from oppression, and for the maintenance of justice and the rights of the kingdom. He was distinguished for his learning; to him an assiduous attention to divine duties was a pleasure; he was moderate and frugal; and it was a usual practice of his to watch by night in preference to sleeping. He was bold in speech, and of severe aspect; he put great confidence in the prayers of religious men, and always paid great respect to ecclesiastics. He endeavoured to adhere to the counsels of St Robert, surnamed Grosstete, bishop of Lincoln, and intrusted his children to him to be brought up, when very young. On that prelate's counsel he relied when arranging matters of difficulty, when attempting dubious enterprises, and in finishing what he had begun, especially in those matters by which he hoped to increase his merits. It was reported that the same bishop had enjoined on him, in order to obtain remission of his sins, to take up this cause, for which he fought even to the death; declaring that the peace of the church in England could not be firmly established except by the sword, and positively assuring him that all who died for it would be crowned with martyrdom. Some persons, moreover, stated, that on one occasion, the bishop placed his hand on the head of the earl's eldest son, and said to him, 'My well-beloved child, both thou and thy father shall die on one day, and by one kind of death; but it will be in the cause of justice and truth.' Report goes, that Simon, after his death, was distinguished by the working of many miracles, which, however, were not made publicly known, for fear of kings.

❖

Edward I

Source: Nicholas Trivet, *Annals*, ed. T. Hog (1845), pp. 281–3, trans. F. M. Powicke, *Henry III and the Lord Edward* (amended)

Edward, king of the English, the first-born of Henry III and Eleanor, daughter of the Count of Provence, was thirty-three years and five months old on the day when his father died and he succeeded to the kingdom. He was a man of tried prudence in the transaction of affairs, devoted from his earliest years to the practice of arms. Hence he had won that fame as a knight in diverse lands which gave him a transcendent place among christian princes. He was handsome, and so tall that he stood head and shoulders above most people. His hair, light and silvery when he was a boy, turned very dark in manhood, and, as he grew old, became as white as a swan. He had a broad brow and symmetrical features, except that a droop of the left eyelid recalled his father's appearance. He was persuasive and ready in speech, in spite of his lisp. His long arms with their powerful and agile play enabled him to become a swordsman second to none; his chest projected beyond his belly, and his long shanks gave him his firm seat in the saddle and his mastery over the most spirited thoroughbred. When he was not fighting, his passions were hawking and the chase, particularly of stag, which he followed on a courser, and slew with his sword, making no use of the trap or buckstall as a hunter.

He was a very fortunate man, protected by the most high God. One day, when he was quite young, he was playing chess with a knight in a vaulted chamber, and, for no particular reason, suddenly arose and went out of the room, whereupon an enormous stone fell just where he had been sitting. On numerous other occasions too he escaped from tight places, and was saved from accidents. He had that greatness of mind which is impatient of injury, heedless of danger in the pursuit of vengeance, yet easily mollified by submission. One day he was hawking by a river and noticed that one of his companions was neglecting to deal with a falcon which had fastened onto a duck among some willows. He expostulated, and when the other still seemed slow to respond, lost his temper and began to threaten him. The stream was between them; no ford or bridge was nearby, and the man flippantly called attention to his immunity. Edward, thoroughly aroused, immediately plunged into the water, not knowing how deep it was, swam his horse across, and in spite of the overhanging bank forced his way out on the other side. He now pursued his companion sword in hand, but when he, despairing of escaping, turned his horse and awaited the blow with bared head Edward checked his horse, sheathed his sword and they returned amicably to deal with the falcon.

❖

Quo Warranto

Source: Statutes of the Realm (1801–28), Vol. I p. 107, quoted T. F. T. Plucknett, The Legislation of Edward I (1949), p. 49

As for the writ called *quo warranto*, our lord the king established on Whit Sunday [1290], the eighteenth year of his reign that all those who claim to have quiet possession of Franchises before the time of King Richard [I], and can show this by a good inquest, may properly enjoy that possession. And if that possession is reasonably demanded, our lord the king will confirm it by title. . . .

❖

The Statute of *Quia Emptores* (1290)

Source: W. Stubbs, *op. cit.,* p. 473, trans. C. Stephenson and F. G. Marcham, p. 174

Whereas the buyers of lands and tenements belonging to the fiefs of magnates and other men have in times past frequently entered upon their fiefs to the prejudice of the same [lords], because the freeholders of the said magnates and other men have sold their lands and tenements to such purchasers to be held in fee by themselves and their heirs of the feoffers and not of the principal lords of the fiefs, whereby those same principal lords have often lost the escheats, marriages and wardships of lands and tenements belonging to their fiefs; and whereas this has seemed very hard and burdensome to those magnates and other lords, being in such cases manifest disinheritance: [therefore] the lord king in his parliament at Westminster [held] after Easter in the eighteenth year of his reign . . . at the suggestion of the magnates of his realm, has granted, provided, and established that henceforth every freeman shall be permitted to sell his land or tenement, or part of it, at pleasure; yet so that the feoffee shall hold that land or tenement of the same principal lord [of whom the feoffer held] and by the same services and customs by which the feoffer earlier held. . . .

The Administration
of Edwardian Justice (1281)

Source: Ancient Correspondence (1902), Vol. XXIV no. 74, quoted
F. M. Powicke, *The Thirteenth Century* (1953), p. 335

Since we fully intend to finish the present eyre in Devon before
Easter [13 April] we beg you[1] to tell us as quickly as you can into
what shire we should adjourn after Easter and to what date, and
whether we must all come to parliament. Please note that if we must
all come the shire of Cornwall cannot be summoned before the week
or fortnight after Trinity [8 June] for the time between Easter week
and parliament is short and it is a long journey from London to
Cornwall, and, as you know, parliament involves much delay. If
you were willing to prorogue the eyre until after Michaelmas, you
would do much service both to the whole shire and to us, for corn
has failed there this year and if we go there in the summer we shall
bring back meagre cheeks. Please let us know your good pleasure
by the bearer. May your reverend lordship ever prosper.

❖

1. Robert Burnell, Chancellor.

The Confirmation of the Charters
(1297)

Source: W. Stubbs, *op. cit.*, p. 490, trans. C. Stephenson and F. G. Marcham, pp. 164–5

Edward, by the grace of God king of England, lord of Ireland and duke of Aquitaine, to all who may see or hear these present letters, greeting. Know that, for the honour of God and of Holy Church, and for the benefit of our entire kingdom, we have granted for ourself and for our heirs that the Great Charter of Liberties and the Charter of the Forest, which were drawn up by the common assent of the whole kingdom in the time of King Henry, our father, are to be observed without impairment in all their particulars. And we will that those same charters shall be sent under our seal to our justices—those of the forest as well as the others—to all sheriffs of counties, and to all our other ministers, as well as to all cities throughout the land, together with our writs providing that the aforesaid charters are to be published and announcement is to be made to the people that we have granted these [charters] to be observed in all their particulars; and that our justices, sheriffs, mayors, and other ministers, whose duty it is to administer the law of the land under us and through our agency, shall cause the same charters in all particulars to be admitted in pleas and judgments before them—that is to say, the Great Charter of Liberties as common law and the Charter of the Forest according to the assize of the forest, for the relief of our people. And we will that, if any judgment is henceforth rendered contrary to the particulars of the charters aforesaid by our justices, or by our other ministers, before whom pleas are held, contrary to the particulars of the charters, it shall be null and void. And we will that these same charters shall be sent under our seal to the cathedral churches throughout the kingdom and shall there remain; and twice a year they shall be read to

19

the people. And [we will] that the archbishops and bishops shall pronounce sentences of greater excommunication against all those who, by deed or aid or counsel, shall violate the aforesaid charters, infringing them in any particular or violating them in any way; and the aforesaid prelates shall pronounce and publish these sentences twice a year. And if the same prelates—the bishops or any of them—prove negligent in making the aforesaid denunciation, by the archbishops of Canterbury and York who at the time hold office, they shall be reproved in a suitable manner and compelled to make this same denunciation in the form aforesaid.

And whereas some people of our kingdom are fearful that the aids and taxes, which by their liberality and goodwill they have heretofore paid to us for the sake of our wars and other needs, shall, despite the nature of the grants, be turned into a servile obligation for them and their heirs because these [payments] may at a future time be found in the rolls, and likewise the prises that in our name have been taken throughout the kingdom by our ministers: [therefore] we have granted, for us and our heirs, that, on account of anything that has been done or that can be found from a roll or in some other way, we will not make into a precedent for the future any such aids, taxes, or prises. And for us and our heirs we have also granted to the archbishops, bishops, abbots, priors, and other folk of Holy Church, and to the earls and barons and the whole community of the land, that on no account will we henceforth take from our kingdom such aids, taxes, and prises, except by the common assent of the whole kingdom and for the common benefit of the same kingdom, saving the ancient aids and prises due and accustomed.

And whereas the greater part of the community all feel themselves gravely oppressed by the maltote on wool—that is to say, 40s from each sack of wool—and have besought us to relieve them [of the charge], at their prayer we have fully relieved them, granting that henceforth we will take neither this nor any other [custom] without their common assent and good will, saving to us and our heirs the custom on wool, wool-fells, and hides previously granted by the community of the kingdom aforesaid.

In testimony whereof we have caused to be written these our letters patent. Given at Ghent, November 5, in the twenty-fifth year of our reign.

❖

Wales

1. EDWARD I'S WELSH TROOPS (1297)

Source: Lodewyk van Veltham, trans. of the Cymmrodorion Society (1925–6), p. 46, quoted F. M. Powicke, *The Thirteenth Century* (1953), p. 384

There you saw the peculiar habits of the Welsh. In the very depth of winter they were running about bare-legged. They wore a red robe. They could not have been warm. The money they received from the king was spent in milk and butter. They would eat and drink anywhere. I never saw them wearing armour. I studied them very closely and walked among them to find out what defensive armour they carried when going into battle. Their weapons were bows, arrows and swords. They had also jardins. They wore linen clothing. They were great drinkers. They endamaged the Flemings very much. Their pay was too small and so it came about that they took what did not belong to them.

2. LLYWELYN WRITES TO EDWARD I (JULY 1273)

Source: Calendar of Ancient Correspondence concerning Wales (1935), p. 86, quoted F. M. Powicke, *Henry III and the Lord Edward* (1947), pp. 621–2

We have received the letter written in the king's name, dated Westminster 20 June, forbidding us to construct a castle on our own land near Aber Miwl, or to establish a town or market there. We are sure that the letter was not issued with your knowledge, and would not have proceeded from the chancery if you had been in your kingdom; for you know well that the rights of our principality are entirely separate from the rights of your kingdom, although we hold our principality under your royal power. You have heard and in part seen that we and our ancestors had the power within our boundaries to build castles and forts and create markets without prohibition by anyone or any announcement of new work. We pray you not to listen to the evil suggestions of those who seek to exasperate your mind against us.

3. EDWARD I WRITES TO LLYWELYN (18 JULY 1280)

Source: op. cit., pp. 59–60, quoted F. M. Powicke *ibid.*, pp. 667–8

The king wishes the peace [the Treaty of Conway 1277] recently made between them to be observed in all its articles, and hopes and believes that Llywelyn for his part will do the same. And because certain matters are contained in that peace which are not yet fully made clear, the king has recently had in his parliament in the presence of Llywelyn's men a long and careful discussion with the prelates and magnates of his realm concerning these matters. The opinion of all was that the king could not in these doubtful matters do otherwise than had hitherto been customary in the days of his predecessors, kings of England . . . Nor by right ought Llywelyn to wonder that the king had recourse to the prelates and magnates of his realm in these as in other matters. Nor in this business of such weight that the king should not always, according to God and justice, do what the prelates and magnates of his realm shall advise, especially as no-one supposes that such prudent men will give the king advice dissonant with or contrary to reason.

Source: The Statute of Wales, *Statutes of the Realm* (1810–28), Vol. I pp. 55–68, quoted F. M. Powicke *ibid.*, p. 663

We . . . being desirous that our aforesaid land of Snowdon and our other lands in those parts, like as all those which are subject unto our power, should be governed with due order . . . to the advancement of justice, and that the people or inhabitants of those lands, who have submitted themselves completely to our will and whom we have thereunto so accepted, should be protected in security within our peace under fixed laws and customs, have caused to be rehearsed before us and the leading men of our realm the laws and customs of those parts hitherto in use: which being diligently heard and fully understood, we have, with the counsel of the aforesaid abolished certain of them, allowed some and corrected some. We have also commanded certain others to be ordained and added thereto. And we wish these laws and customs to be kept and observed in perpetuity in our lands in those parts, in the form written below. . .

❖

Scotland

I. THE SOVEREIGNTY OF SCOTLAND (1291)

Source: A Source Book of Scottish History, ed. W. C. Dickinson, G. Donaldson and I. A. Milne (1952), Vol. I p. 113

. . . To all who shall see or hear these letters, Florence Count of Holland, Robert de Brus Lord of Annandale, John Balliol Lord of Galloway, John de Hastings Lord of Abergavenny, John Comyn Lord of Badenoughe, Patrik de Dunbar Earl of the March, John de

Vesey for his father, Nicolas de Soules and William de Ros, greeting in God.

Seeing that we profess to have right to the kingdom of Scotland, and to set forth, maintain and declare such rights before that person who has most power, jurisdiction and reason to try our right; and the noble Prince, Sir Edward by the grace of God King of England, has shown to us, by good and sufficient reasons, that to him belongs, and that he ought to have, the sovereign lordship of the said kingdom of Scotland, and the cognizance of hearing, trying and determining our right; We, of our own will, without any manner of force or constraint, will, concede and grant to receive justice before him as sovereign lord of the land; and we are willing, moreover, and promise to have and hold firm and stable his act, and that he shall have the realm, to whom right shall give it before him. In witness of this thing we have put our seals to this writing. Made and given at Norham, the Tuesday next after the Ascension, the year of grace one thousand two hundred and ninety-first.

2. THE DEATH OF WILLIAM WALLACE

Source: Matthew of Westminster, *The Flowers of History*, ed. H. R. Luard (1890), Vol. III pp. 123–4

Wilielmus Waleis, a man void of pity, a robber given to sacrilege, arson and homicide, more hardened in cruelty than Herod, more raging in madness than Nero . . . was condemned to a most cruel but justly deserved death. He was drawn through the streets of London at the tails of horses, until he reached a gallows of unusual height, especially prepared for him; there he was suspended by a halter; but taken down while yet alive, he was mutilated, his bowels torn out and burned in a fire, his head then cut off, his body divided into four, and his quarters transmitted to four principal parts of Scotland. Behold the end of the merciless man, who himself perishes without mercy.

Source: Life of Edward II, ed. N. Denholm-Young (1957), pp. 50-1

When all necessaries had been collected, the king and the other magnates of the land with a great multitude of carts and baggage-wagons set out for Scotland. When the lord king had reached Berwick, he made a short halt there to await the arrival of the army. But the Earl of Lancaster, the Earl Warenne, the Earl of Arundel, and the Earl of Warwick did not come, but sent knights equipped to do their due service for them in the army. On the sixth and seventh day before the feast of St John the Baptist, our king with all his army left Berwick and took his way towards Stirling. The cavalry numbered more than two thousand, without counting a numerous crowd of infantry. There were in that company quite sufficient to penetrate the whole of Scotland, and some thought if the whole strength of Scotland had been gathered together, they would not have stayed to face the king's army. Indeed all who were present agreed that never in our time has such an army gone forth from England. The multitude of wagons if they had been placed end to end, would have taken up a space of twenty leagues.

The king therefore took confidence and courage from so great and so distinguished a multitude and hastened day by day to the appointed place, not as if he was leading an army to battle but as if he was going to St James's [of Compostella]. Brief were the halts for sleep, briefer still for food; hence horses, horsemen and infantry were worn out with toil and hunger, and if they did not bear themselves well it was hardly their fault.

4. THE BATTLE OF BANNOCKBURN (1314)

Source: The Chronicle of Lanercost, trans. H. Maxwell (1913), p. 207

On the morrow—an evil, miserable and calamitous day for the English—when both sides had made themselves ready for battle, the English archers were thrown forward before the line, and the

Scottish archers engaged them, a few being killed or wounded on either side; but the King of England's archers quickly put the others to flight. Now when the two armies had approached very near each other, all the Scots fell on their knees to repeat *Pater-Noster*, commending themselves to God and seeking help from heaven; after which they advanced boldly against the English. They had so arranged their army that two columns went abreast in advance of the third, so that neither should be in advance of the other; and the third followed, in which was Robert [Bruce]. Of a truth, when both armies engaged each other, and the great horses of the English charged the pikes of the Scots, as it were into a dense forest, there arose a great and terrible crash of spears broken and of destriers wounded to the death; and so they remained without movement for a while. Now the English in the rear could not reach the Scots because the leading division was in the way, nor could they do anything to help themselves, wherefore there was nothing for it but to take to flight. This account I have heard from a trustworthy person who was present as eyewitness.

In the leading division were killed the Earl of Gloucester, Sir John Comyn, Sir Pagan de Typtoft, Sir Edmund de Mauley and many other nobles, besides foot soldiers who fell in great numbers. Another calamity which befell the English was that, whereas they had shortly before crossed a great ditch called Bannockburn, into which the tide flows, and now wanted to recross it in confusion, many nobles and others fell into it with their horses in the crush, while others escaped with much difficulty, and many were never able to extricate themselves from the ditch; thus Bannockburn was spoken about for many years in English throats.

5 . THE STONE OF SCONE

Source: Life of Edward II, ed. N. Denholm-Young (1957), p. 132

The Scots also demanded that the royal stone should be restored to them, which Edward I had long ago taken from Scotland and placed at Westminster by the tomb of St Edward. This stone was of famous memory amongst the Scots, because upon it the kings of Scotland used to receive the symbols of authority and the Sceptre. Scota, daughter of Pharaoh, brought this stone with her from the borders of Egypt when she landed in Scotland and subdued the land. For Moses had prophesied that whoever bore that stone with him should bring broad lands under the yoke of his lordship. Whence from Scota the land is called Scotland which was formerly called Albany from Albanactus.

✦

Edward II and the Ordainers

I. EDWARD II

Source: op. cit., pp. 39–40

For our King Edward has now reigned six full years and has till now achieved nothing praiseworthy or memorable, except that by a royal marriage he has raised up for himself a handsome son and heir to the throne. How differently began King Richard's reign: before the end of the third year of his reign he had scattered far and wide the rays of his valour. In one day he took Messina, a city of Sicily, by force, and subdued the land of Cyprus in a fortnight. Then, how he bore himself at Acre and in other foreign parts history vividly relates in the Latin and French tongues. Oh! If our king Edward had borne himself as well at the outset of his reign, and not accepted the counsels of wicked men, not one of his predecessors would have been more notable than he. For God had endowed him with every gift, and had made him equal to or indeed more excellent than other kings. If anyone dared to describe those qualities which ennoble our king, he would not find his like in the land. His ancestry, reaching back to the tenth generation, shows his nobility. At the beginning of his reign he was rich, with a populous land and the goodwill of his people. He became the son-in-law of the King of France, and first cousin of the King of Spain. If he had followed the advice of the barons he would have humiliated the Scots with ease. If he had habituated himself to the use of arms, he would have exceeded the prowess of King Richard. Physically this would have been inevitable, for he was tall and strong, a fine figure of a handsome man. But why linger over this description? If only he had given to arms the labour that he expended on rustic pursuits, he would have raised England aloft; his name would have resounded through the land. What hopes he raised as Prince of Wales! How they were dashed when he became King!

2. CORONATION OATH OF EDWARD II (1308)

Source: Statutes of the Realm (1810–28), Vol. I p. 168, trans. C. Stephenson and F. G. Marcham, *op. cit.*, p. 192

'Sire, will you grant and keep and by your oath confirm to the people of England the laws and customs given to them by the previous just and god-fearing kings, your ancestors, and especially the laws, customs, and liberties granted to the clergy and people by the glorious king, the sainted Edward, your predecessor?' 'I grant and promise them.'

'Sire, will you in all your judgments, so far as in you lies, preserve to God and Holy Church, and to the people and clergy, entire peace and concord before God?' 'I will preserve them.'

'Sire, will you, so far as in you lies, cause justice to be rendered rightly, impartially, and wisely, in compassion and in truth?' 'I will do so.'

'Sire, do you grant to be held and observed the just laws and customs that the community of your realm shall determine, and will you, so far as in you lies, defend and strengthen them to the honour of God?' 'I grant and promise them.'

3. PIERS GAVESTON

Source: Life of Edward II, ed. N. Denholm-Young (1957), pp. 14–15

This Piers originated in Gascony, the son of a certain knight who had been of the household of the elder king Edward. While Edward the younger was still Prince of Wales, the said Piers was received into his household as a young esquire, and by a gratifying attention to his duties he quickly found the highest favour in his master's sight. And, to make a long story short, our king when he had obtained the kingdom on the death of his father, made Piers de Gaveston Earl of Cornwall. But Piers now Earl of Cornwall did not wish to remember that he had once been Piers the humble esquire. For Piers accounted no one his fellow, no one his peer, save the king alone. Indeed his countenance exacted greater deference than that of the king. His arrogance was intolerable to the barons and a prime cause of hatred and rancour. For it is commonly said,

> You may be rich and wise and handsome,
> But insolence could be your ruin.

I therefore believe and firmly maintain that if Piers had from the outset borne himself prudently and humbly towards the magnates of the land, none of them would ever have opposed him. But there was a secondary cause of their hatred, namely that, though of old it has been desirable for all men to find favour in the eyes of kings, Piers alone received a gracious welcome from the king and enjoyed his favour to such an extent that if an earl or baron entered the king's chamber to speak with the king, in Piers' presence the king addressed no-one, and to none showed a friendly countenance save to Piers only. And in truth it is from such-like behaviour that envy frequently springs. Indeed I do not remember to have heard that one man so loved another. Jonathan cherished David, Achilles loved Patroclus. But we do not read that they were immoderate. Our king, however, was incapable of moderate favour, and on account of Piers was said to forget himself, and so Piers was accounted a sorcerer.

4. THOMAS, EARL OF LANCASTER

Source: op. cit., pp. 28–9

This Earl Thomas was related to the king in the second degree of kinship, for they were descended from two brothers in the first degree, to wit King Edward the elder, and his brother Edmund, Earl of Lancaster. His mother was Queen of Navarre, his sister Queen of France, and his sister's daughter now Queen of England. As each parent was of royal birth he was clearly of nobler descent than the other earls. By the size of his patrimony you may assess his influence. For he had five earldoms in England, namely those of Lancaster, Leicester, and Ferrers from his father, and the earldoms of Lincoln and Salisbury from his wife. See how the lordship of so many noble earldoms is now reduced to one. Thomas alone can now achieve as much as formerly Earl Edmund, the Lord Longespee, the Lord Lucy, and the Lord Ferrers, four separate lords. Nor do I believe that any duke or count under the Roman empire, received as much from the profits of his lands as Thomas Earl of Lancaster.

5. THE ORDINANCES OF 1311

Source: Statutes of the Realm (1810–28), Vol. I p. 157, trans. C. Stephenson and F. G. Marcham, *op. cit.*, pp. 193–8

Whereas, through bad and deceitful counsel, our lord the king and all his men have everywhere been dishonoured and his crown in many ways has been debased and ruined, while his lands of Gascony, Ireland and Scotland are on the point of being lost unless God improves the situation, and his realm of England has been brought to the verge of rebellion through prises and [other] oppressive and destructive measures—which facts are known and proved —our lord the king of his free will has granted to the prelates, earls, and barons, and to the other good men of his realm, that certain persons should be elected to ordain and determine the condition of his household and of his realm, as appears more fully in the commission issued by our lord the king in this connection. Therefore we, Robert, by the grace of God archbishop of Canterbury and primate of all England, and the bishops, earls, and barons elected by virtue of the said commission, do ordain for the honour of God and Holy Church and of the king and his realm in the manner following:

i. In the first place it is ordained that Holy Church shall have all its liberties as heretofore and as it should have them.

ii. Item, it is ordained that the king's peace shall be firmly kept throughout the entire kingdom, so that every one may safely go, come, and remain according to the law and custom of the realm.

iii. Item, it is ordained that, in order to acquit the king's debts, to relieve his estate, and the more honourably to maintain it, no gift of land, rent, liberty, escheat, wardship, marriage, or office shall be made to any of the said Ordainers during their power under the said ordinance, or to any other person, without the counsel and assent of the said Ordainers or the majority of them—or of six of them at least—but that all sources of profit shall be improved for the benefit of the king until his estate is properly relieved and some other ordinance may be made for the honour and profit of the king.

iv. Item, it is ordained that the customs of the kingdom shall be received and kept by men of the kingdom itself, and not by aliens; and that the issues and profits of the same customs, together with all other issues and profits pertaining to the kingdom from any source whatsoever, shall in their entirety come to the king's exchequer and be paid by the treasurer and the chamberlains for maintaining the king's household and in other ways for his benefit; so that the king may live of his own without taking prises other than those anciently due and accustomed. And all others shall cease. . . .

vi. Item, it is ordained that the Great Charter shall be observed in all its particulars; so that, if there is any point in the said charter that is doubtful or obscure, it shall be interpreted by the said Ordainers and other men whom they may see fit to call upon for that purpose.

vii. And besides, since the crown has been so abased and ruined by numerous grants, we ordain that all grants made to the damage of the king and the impoverishment of the crown since the commission was given to us ... shall be annulled; and we do annul them entirely, so that they shall not be given back to the same persons without the common assent [of the baronage] in parliament. . . .

ix. Whereas the king, on account of the many perils that he and his kingdom may incur, ought not to undertake an act of war against any one, or to go out of the kingdom, without the common assent of his baronage, we ordain that henceforth the king shall neither go out of the kingdom nor undertake an act of war against any one without the common assent of his baronage, and that in parliament. . . .

x. And whereas it is feared that the people of the land will rebel on account of the prises and divers oppressions recently established, ... we ordain that henceforth all prises shall be abolished except the ancient and lawful prises due to the king and to others who are lawfully entitled to them. And if any prises are taken contrary to the ordinance aforesaid by any one whomsoever, no matter of what condition he may be—that is to say, if any one, under colour of purveyance for the use of our lord the king or of some one else, takes grain, wares, merchandise, or other goods against the will of those to whom they belong, and does not immediately give in return money to the true value, unless he thereof has respite by the free will of the seller according to the provision in the Great Charter regarding prises taken by constables of castles and their bailiffs, saving the accustomed prises aforesaid—notwithstanding any commission that may be [issued], pursuit with hue and cry shall be raised against him and he shall be taken to the nearest jail of the king, and the common law shall be enforced against him as against a robber or thief, should he be convicted of such.

xi. Also, [whereas] new customs have been levied and the old have been increased upon wool, cloth, wines, avoirdupois, and other things—whereby [our] merchants come more rarely and bring fewer goods into the country, while alien merchants reside longer than they used to be, to the damage of the king and his people—we ordain that all manner of customs and maltotes levied since the coronation of King Edward, son of King Henry, are to be entirely removed and utterly abolished forever, notwithstanding the charter which the said King Edward granted to alien merchants, because it was issued contrary to the Great Charter and contary to the liberty of the city of London and without the assent of the baronage.

xii. And whereas the king, as aforesaid, has been badly advised and guided by evil counsellors, we ordain that all the evil counsellors shall be put out and utterly removed, so that neither they nor other such persons shall be near him or shall be retained in any office under the king; and that other persons who are fit shall be put in their places. And the same shall be done in the case of domestics, officials, and other men in the king's household who are not fit.

xiv. And whereas many evils have been incurred through such councillors and such ministers, we ordain that the king shall appoint the chancellor, the chief justices of both benches, the treasurer, the chancellor and the chief baron of the exchequer, the steward of the household, the keeper of the wardrobe, the comptroller and a fit clerk to keep the privy seal, a chief keeper of the forests on this side of Trent and one on the other side of Trent, also an escheator on this side of Trent and one on the other side, as well as the king's chief clerk of the common bench, by the counsel and assent of the baronage, and that in parliament. And if by some chance it happens that there is need to appoint any of the said ministers before parliament meets, then the king shall make such appointments by the good counsel whom he shall have near him up to the time of the parliament. And so let it be done henceforth with regard to such ministers whenever there is need.

xv. Item, we ordain that the chief wardens of ports and of castles on the sea shall be appointed and installed in the aforesaid manner, and that such wardens are to be of the land itself.

xvi. And whereas the lands of Gascony, Ireland and Scotland are in peril of being lost through default of good ministers, we ordain that worthy and fit ministers to keep ward in the said lands shall be named according to the form set forth in the article before the last.

xvii. Moreover, we ordain that sheriffs shall henceforth be appointed by the chancellor, the treasurer, and other of the council who are present; and if the chancellor is not present, let them be appointed by the treasurer, the barons of the exchequer, and the justices of the bench. And such men are to be named and installed as are fit and worthy, and as have lands and tenements through which they may be held responsible for their actions to the king or to the people. And only such persons shall be appointed, and they shall have their commissions under the great seal. . . .

xxiv. And whereas the people feel much aggrieved because of divers debts demanded of them for the king's use by summons from the exchequer, of which debts, being actually paid, the people have various acquittances . . . we ordain that henceforth in the account of every sheriff, or other minister of the king who is answerable at the exchequer, such tallies, writs, and franchises as are allowable in the account shall be allowed . . . And if the treasurer and the barons of the exchequer do not act in the manner aforesaid, the plaintiffs shall enjoy recovery through petition in parliament.

xxv. Whereas ordinary merchants and many others of the people are allowed to bring pleas of debt and trespass in the exchequer, through the fact that they are received by the ministers of the said court more favourably than they should be—whereby accounts and other concerns of the king are greatly delayed and, in addition, a large number of people are aggrieved—we ordain that henceforth no pleas shall be held in the said court of the exchequer except pleas touching the king and his ministers: [namely] those answerable at the exchequer by reason of their offices, the ministers of the court itself, and their subordinates and servants who most of the time are with them in those places where the exchequer may be. And if anybody is received by the said court with permission to plead in the manner aforesaid, those impleaded shall have their recovery in parliament.

xvi. Item, whereas the people feel much aggrieved because stewards and marshals hold many pleas that do not pertain to their offices, and also because they will not receive attorneys for defendants as well as for plaintiffs, we ordain that henceforth they shall receive attorneys for defendants as well as for plaintiffs, and that they shall hold no pleas of freehold, debt, covenant or contract, nor any common plea touching men of the people—saving only trespasses of the household itself and other trespasses committed within

34

the verge, and contracts and covenants which any one of the king's household may make with another of the same household within the household itself and not elsewhere. . . .

xxviii. Whereas the people feel much aggrieved because men are emboldened to kill and rob by the fact that the king, through evil counsel, so lightly grants them his peace against the provisions of the law, we ordain that henceforth no felon or fugitive shall be protected or defended in any sort of felony by the king's charter granting his peace, except only in case the king can give grace according to his oath, and that by process of law and the custom of the realm. And if any charter is henceforth made and granted to any one in any other manner, it shall be of no avail and shall be held as null. And no recognized malefactor against the crown and the peace of the land is to be aided or maintained by any one.

xxix. Whereas in the king's court persons find their cases delayed because a party alleges that in the king's absence answer should not be made to demands, and also many persons wrongfully suffer injuries from the king's ministers, with regard to which injuries one can secure recovery only in common parliament; we ordain that the king shall hold a parliament once a year, or twice if need be, and that in a convenient place. And that in those parliaments pleas which are delayed in the said manner, and pleas wherein the justices are of different opinions, shall be recorded and settled. And likewise those bills which are brought to parliament shall be settled as heretofore in accordance with law and right.

xxx. Whereas all the people suffer greatly in many ways whenever a change of money is made in the kingdom, we ordain that, when there is a need and the king wishes to make a change, he shall do so by the common counsel of his baronage, and that in parliament.

xxxi. Item, we ordain that all statutes which were made in amendment of the law and for the benefit of the people by the ancestors of our lord the king shall be kept and maintained as heretofore in accordance with law and right; provided that they are not contrary to the Great Charter or to the Forest Charter or to the ordinances by us made. And if any statute is made contrary to what has been said, it shall be held as null and as utterly void.

xxxii. Whereas, to the great injury of the people, the law of the land and common right have often been delayed by letters issued under the king's privy seal, we ordain that henceforth neither the law of the land nor common right shall be delayed or disturbed by letters under the said seal. And if, through such letters issued under the privy seal contrary to right or to the law of the land, anything is done in any session of the court of our lord the king, it shall be o no avail and shall be held as null.

xxxiii. Whereas many of the people other than those known to be merchants feel much aggrieved and injured by the Statute of Merchants made at Acton Burnell, we ordain that hereafter this statute shall hold only as between merchant and merchant and with regard to dealings made between them. . . .

xxxviii. Item, we ordain that the Great Charter of Liberties and the Forest Charter issued by King Henry, son of King John, shall be observed in all their particulars, and that points in the said charters of liberties which are doubtful shall be explained in the next parliament after this by the advice of the baronage, the justices, and other persons learned in the law. And this is to be done because we are unable to attend to the matter during our term.

xxxix. Item, we ordain that the chancellor, the treasurer, the chief justices of both benches, the chancellor of the exchequer, the keeper of the wardrobe, the steward of the king's household, and all justices, sheriffs, escheators, constables, investigators for any cause whatsoever, and all other bailiffs and ministers of the king, whenever they receive their offices and bailiwicks, shall be sworn to keep and observe all the ordinances made by the prelates, earls, and barons for that purpose elected and assigned—every one of those without contravening them in any particular.

xl. Item, we ordain that in each parliament one bishop, two earls, and two barons shall be assigned to hear and determine all plaints of those wishing to complain of the king's ministers, whichever they may be, who have contravened the ordinances aforesaid. And if the said bishop, earls and barons cannot all attend, or are prevented from hearing and determining the said plaints, then two or three of them shall do so. And those who are found to have contravened the said ordinances, in the interest of the king and in the interest of the plaintiffs, shall be punished at the discretion of the persons thus assigned.

xli. Item, we ordain that the aforesaid ordinances are to be maintained and observed in all their particulars, and that our lord the king shall cause them to be issued under his great seal and sent into every county of England, to be published, held, and strictly kept as well within franchises as without.

These ordinances, having been shown to us and published on Monday next before the feast of St Michael just past, we agree to, accept, and confirm. And we will and grant, for us and our heirs, that all and several of the said ordinances, made according to the form of our letters aforesaid, shall be published throughout our entire realm, henceforth to be strictly maintained and observed. In testimony whereof we have caused these our letters patent to be drawn up.

Given at London, October 5, in the fifth year of our reign.

6. THE REVOCATION OF THE ORDINANCES (1322)

Source: op. cit., Vol. I p. 189, trans. Stephenson/Marcham, pp. 204–5

The which ordinance our said lord the king, at his parliament at York, in three weeks from Easter in the fifteenth year of his reign, did, by the prelates, earls, and barons, among whom were the more part of the said Ordainers who were then living, and by the commonalty of his realm, there by his command assembled, cause to be rehearsed and examined: and forasmuch as upon that examination it was found, in the said parliament, that by the matters so ordained the royal power of our said lord the king was restrained in divers things, contrary to what ought to be, to the blemishing of his royal sovereignty, and against the estate of the crown; and also, forasmuch as if, in times past, by such ordinances and provisions, made by subjects against the royal power of the ancestors of our lord the king, troubles and wars have happened in the realm, whereby the land hath been in peril, it is recorded and established, at the said parliament, by our lord the king, and by the said prelates, earls, and barons, and the whole commonalty of the realm, at this parliament assembled, that all the things, by the said ordainers ordained and contained in the said ordinances, shall from henceforth for the time to come cease and shall lose their name, force, virtue, and effect for ever; the statutes and establishments duly made by our lord the king and his ancestors, before the said ordinances, abiding in their force: and that forever hereafter, all manner of ordinances or provisions, made by the subjects of our lord the king or of his heirs, by any power or authority whatsoever, concerning the royal power of our lord the king or of his heirs, or against the estate of our said lord the king or of his heirs, or against the estate of the crown, shall be void and of no avail or force whatever; but the matters which are to be established for the estate of our lord the king and of his heirs, and for the estate of the realm and of the people, shall be treated, accorded and established in parliaments, by our lord the king, and by the assent of the prelates, earls, and barons, and the commonalty of the realm; according as it hath been heretofore accustomed.

7. THE ARTICLES OF ACCUSATION AGAINST EDWARD II (1327)

Source: Select Documents of English Constitutional History, ed. G. B. Adams and H. M. Stephens (1919), p. 99

It has been decided that prince Edward, the eldest son of the king, shall have the government of the realm and shall be crowned king, for the following reasons:

1. First, because the king is incompetent to govern in person. For throughout his reign he has been controlled and governed by others who have given him evil counsel, to his own dishonour and to the destruction of holy Church and of all his people, without his being willing to see or understand what is good or evil or to make amendment, or his being willing to do as was required by the great and wise men of his realm, or to allow amendment to be made.

2. Item, throughout his reign he has not been willing to listen to good counsel nor to adopt it nor to give himself to the good govern-

ment of his realm, but he has always given himself up to unseemly works and occupations, neglecting to satisfy the needs of his realm.

3. Item, through the lack of good government he has lost the realm of Scotland and other territories and lordships in Gascony and Ireland which his father left him in peace, and he has lost the friendship of the king of France and of many other great men.

4. Item, by his pride and obstinacy and by evil counsel he has destroyed holy Church and imprisoned some of the persons of holy Church and brought distress upon others and also many great and noble men of his land he has put to a shameful death, imprisoned, exiled, and disinherited.

5. Item, wherein he was bound by his oath to do justice to all, he has not willed to do it, for his own profit and his greed and that of the evil councillors who have been about him, nor has he kept the other points of his oath which he made at his coronation, as he was bound to do.

6. Item, he has stripped his realm, and done all that he could to ruin his realm and his people, and what is worse, by his cruelty and lack of character he has shown himself incorrigible without hope of amendment, which things are so notorious that they cannot be denied.

8. THE ABDICATION OF EDWARD II (1327)

Source: Sources of English Constitutional History, trans. C. Stephenson and F. G. Marcham (1937), p. 205

Whereas Sire Edward, recently king of England, of his free will and by the common counsel and assent of the prelates, earls, barons, and other nobles, and of the whole community of the realm, has abdicated the government of the realm; and whereas he has granted and wills that the government of the realm should devolve upon his eldest son and heir, Sire Edward, who should govern, reign, and be crowned king; and whereas all the great men have performed their homage [to the said heir]: we proclaim and publish the peace of our said lord, Sire Edward, the son [of King Edward]; and on his part we command and firmly enjoin each and every one, on pain of disherison and loss of life or members, not to break the peace of our said lord the king; for he is and shall be ready to enforce right for each and every one of the said kingdom in all matters and against all persons, both great and small. So, if any one has some demand to make of another, let him make it by means of [legal] action, without resorting to force or violence.

❖

The Young Edward III writes to the Pope (1330)

Source: The English Church in the Fourteenth Century, W. A. Pantin (1962), pp. 77–8

Most Holy Father, because it will behove us many times to send letters to your Holiness, not only for Our own needs, but also for the advancement of the people of Our household and for others, and on this matter We are informed by My Lord William de Montagne that You will be pleased to have from Us some private countersign by which You can tell which petitions we have tenderly at heart, and which not; We affectionately beseech Your Holiness that the petitions which We shall send You in future by Our letters in Latin or French, sealed under our Privy Seal or under our Signet, on which shall be written in Our hand '*Pater Sancte*'—that these you will please to have specially recommended and You will understand for a certainty that We have them at heart; for our intention is not to press You over these matters by this sign, but to use it at least where we can and as we ought to; and know Most Holy Father, that this matter is not known to anyone except to My Lord William aforesaid and to Master Richard de Bury Our secretary, of whom We are certain that they will keep it secret in every event.

This document was written by the hand of the said Master Richard, for by reason of diverse occupations that We had at the time of despatch of these letters, We could not devote Ourselves to so much writing.

Pater Sancte

❖

The Fall of Mortimer (1330)

Source: Rotuli Parliamentorum (1767), Vol. II pp. 52–3, trans. C. Stephenson and F. G. Marcham, *op. cit.*, pp. 207–8

Our said lord the king charges you, earls and barons, the peers of the realm, that, with regard to these matters vitally affecting him and you and all the people of the kingdom, you render for the said Roger such right and lawful judgment as should be incurred by a man of this sort, who, as he believes, is truly guilty of all the crimes set forth above; and that the said matters are notorious and known to be true to you and all the people of the kingdom.

The which earls, barons, and peers, having examined the articles, returned to the king's presence in the same parliament and all declared through one of the peers that all the matters contained in the said articles were notorious, being known to them and to the people, and especially the article touching the death of Sire Edward, father of our lord the present king. Wherefore, as judges of parliament, the said earls, barons, and peers, by the assent of the king in the same parliament, awarded and adjudged that the said Roger as a traitor and enemy to the king and to the kingdom, should be drawn and hanged. And thereupon the earl marshal was commanded to carry out the execution of the said judgment; and the mayor, aldermen, and sheriffs of London, also the constable of the Tower and those who had [the prisoner] in custody, to be of assistance to the said earl marshal in carrying out the said execution. Which execution was carried out and performed on Thursday next after the first day of parliament, namely, November 29.

❖

The Statute of Treasons (1352)

Source: Statutes of the Realm (1810–28), Vol. I p. 319, trans. C. Stephenson and F. G. Marcham, *op. cit.*, p. 227

. . . Item, whereas until now there have been various opinions as to which cases should be called treason and which not, the king, at the request of the lords and the commons, has made the following declarations:

If a man compasses or imagines the death of our lord the king, of our lady his consort, or of their eldest son and heir; or if a man violates the king's consort, the king's eldest daughter being as yet unmarried, or the consort of the king's eldest son and heir; or if a man makes war against our said lord the king in his kingdom, or is an adherent of enemies to our lord the king in the kingdom, giving them aid or comfort in his kingdom or elsewhere . . .; or if a man counterfeits the great or the privy seal of the king or his money; or if a man, for the sake of trading or making payments in deceit of our said lord the king or his people, brings into this kingdom false coin, counterfeit of the money of England . . . knowing it to be false; or if a man slays the chancellor, treasurer, or justice of our lord the king . . . while [such official is] in his place and attending to his office—these cases specified above, it must be understood, are to be adjudged treason against our lord the king and his royal majesty; and in such [cases of] treason forfeiture of property pertains to our lord the king, as well lands and tenements held of another as those held of [the king] himself. . . .

❖

A Threat to depose Richard II (1386)

Source: Henry Knighton, ed. J. R. Lumby (1889–95), Vol. II p. 219, trans. G. B. Adams and H. M. Stephens, *op. cit.*

Yet one other thing remains of our message for us to announce to you on the part of your people. For they have it from an old statute, and in fact not very long ago put into force, which is to be regretted, that if the king from any malignant design or foolish contumacy or contempt or wanton wilfulness or in any irregular way should alienate himself from his people, and should not be willing to be governed and regulated by the laws, statutes and laudable ordinances of the realm with the wholesome advice of the lords and peers of the realm, but should headily and wantonly by his own mad designs work out his own private purpose, then it should be lawful for them with the common assent and consent of the people of the realm to depose the king himself from the royal throne and to elevate to the royal throne in his place some near kinsman of the royal line.

✦

Ordinance concerning the King's Council (1390)

Source: Proceedings of the Privy Council, ed. H. Nicolas (1834–7), Vol. I p. 18, trans. C. Stephenson and F. G. Marcham, *op. cit.,* pp. 244–5

In the first place, the lords of the council shall take pains to appear at a council by eight or nine o'clock at the latest.

Item, the affairs of the king and the kingdom are to be examined in preference to all others when the greater men of the council and the other officers are present.

Item, matters touching the common law are to be sent for determination before the justices.

Item, matters touching the office of chancellor are to be sent for determination before him in the chancery.

Item, matters touching the office of treasurer are to be sent for determination before him in the exchequer.

Item, all other matters, which cannot be settled without the special grace and permission of the king, are to be laid before him in order thereon to have his opinion and pleasure.

Item, no gift or grant that may be turned to the diminution of the king's profit shall be passed without the advice of the council and the assent of the dukes of Guienne, York, and Gloucester, and of the chancellor, or of two of them.

Item, all other matters presented to the council in order to have their advice, and other matters of great weight, are to be determined by those of the council who are present, together with the officers.

Item, all other bills of less weight from the people are to be examined and determined before the keeper of the privy seal and others of the council who may be present at the time.

Item, ordinances previously made by the assent of the king and of his council with regard to offices in his gift are to be held and observed.

Item, no steward or justice is henceforth to be appointed for the term of his life.

Item, bachelors who are of the king's council shall have reasonable wages for the time spent in work connected with the same council.

Item, lords who are of the same council shall receive consideration for their labour and expense by the advice of the king and his council.

Item, after one matter has been introduced in the council, they shall not pass on to any other matter until an answer has been given in the matter first introduced.

On March 8, in the thirteenth year, etc., this ordinance was made at Westminster in the presence of the king, there being in attendance the duke of Guienne, the duke of York, the earl of Salisbury, the earl of Northumberland, the earl of Huntingdon, the chancellor, the treasurer, the keeper of the privy seal, the steward, Lovell, Stury, and Dalynrigg.

✦

The Abdication of Richard II (1399)

Source: Rotuli Parliamentorum (1767), Vol. III p. 416, trans G. B. Adams and H. M. Stephens, *op. cit.*

In God's name, Amen. I, Richard, by the grace of God, king of England and France, and lord of Ireland, absolve all archbishops and bishops of the said kingdoms and lordships, and all other prelates whatsoever of secular or regular churches of whatsoever dignity, rank, state, or condition they may be, and dukes, marquises, earls, barons, knights, vassals, and vavassors and all my liege men, clerical or secular by whatsoever name they are known, from the oath of fealty and homage and all others whatsoever made to me and from every bond of allegiance, royalty and lordship with which they have been or are bound by oath to me, or bound in any other way whatsoever, and these and their heirs and successors in per- petuity from these bonds and oaths and all other bonds whatsoever, I relieve, free, and excuse; absolved, excused and freed as far as per- tains to my person, I release them from every performance of their oaths which could follow from their promises or from any of them; and all royal dignity and majesty and royalty and also the lordship and power in the said realms and lordship; and my other lordships and possessions or whatsoever others belong to me in any way, under whatsoever name they are known, which are in the aforesaid realms and lordships or elsewhere; and all right and colour of right, and titles, possessions and lordship which I have ever had, still have or shall be able to have in any way, in these or any of them, or to these with their rights and everything pertaining to them or dependent upon them in any way whatsoever; from these or any of them, and also the command, government, and administration of such realms and lordships; and all and every kind of absolute and mixed sovereignty and jurisdiction in these realms and lordships belonging to me or to belong to me; the name and honour and royal right and title of king, freely, voluntarily, unequivocally, and absolutely, and in the best fashion, wise, and form possible, in these writings I renounce and resign as a whole, and release in word and deed, and yield my place in them, and retire from them forever.

Saving to my successors, kings of England, in the realms and lordships and all other premises in perpetuity, the rights belonging or to belong to them, in them, or in any of them, I confess, acknowledge, consider, and truly judge from sure knowledge that I in the rule and government of the said realms and lordships and all pertaining to them have been and am wholly insufficient and useless, and because of my notorious deserts am not unworthy to be deposed. And I swear on these holy gospels touched bodily by me that I will never contravene these premises of renunciation, resignation, demise and surrender, nor will I impugn them in any way, in deed or in word by myself or by another or others, or as far as in me lies permit them to be contravened or impugned publicly or secretly, but I will hold this renunciation, resignation, demise, and surrender unalterable and acceptable and I will keep it firmly and observe it in whole and in every part, so may God help me and these holy scriptures of God. I, Richard, the aforesaid king, subscribe myself with my own hand.

The Succession of Henry IV

Source: Rotuli Parliamentorum (1767), Vol. III pp. 415–34, trans. C. Stephenson and F. G. Marcham, *op. cit.*, pp. 250–5

At the Parliament summoned and held at Westminster by King Henry IV on Monday, the day of St Faith the Virgin . . . in the presence of the same king seated on his royal throne in the great hall of Westminster, and of all the lords spiritual and temporal, and of the commons who had come thither by virtue of their summons to parliament, and of many other gentlemen and commoners there present in large numbers, Thomas of Arundel, archbishop of Canterbury, related how King Richard II after the Conquest had summoned his parliament to be held there on the previous Tuesday . . .; which summons was without force and effect through the acceptance of the renunciation made by the same King Richard, and through the deposition of the same King Richard made on the aforesaid Tuesday, as more fully appears in the record and process drawn up in this connection and enrolled in this roll of parliament. . . .

. . . in the great hall at Westminster, honourably prepared for the holding of parliament, in the presence of the said archbishops of Canterbury and York, of the Duke of Lancaster, of other dukes and lords both spiritual and temporal whose names are inscribed below, and of the people of the said kingdom then and there assembled in a very great multitude for the sake of [witnessing] the deeds of parliament, while the aforesaid duke of Lancaster occupied the place due and accustomed to his estate and while the royal throne, solemnly prepared with cloth of gold, stood vacant in the absence of any presiding officer whatsoever, the aforesaid archbishop of York . . . had the said cession and renunciation read by another, first in Latin and then in English. And immediately it was asked of the estates and the people then and there present . . . whether for their own interest and for the benefit of the kingdom, they wished to accept the same renunciation and cession. And the same estates and people, considering, for the reasons specified by the king himself in his aforesaid renunciation and cession, that to do so would be highly expedient, all singly and in common with the people unanimously and with one accord accepted such renunciation and cession. After this acceptance, however, it was then publicly set forth that, besides the renunciation and cession accepted as aforesaid, it would in many ways be expedient and advantageous for the said kingdom if, in order to obviate all scruple and evil suspicion, the many crimes and defaults frequently committed by the said king in connection with the bad government of his kingdom—on account of which, as he himself had asserted in the cession made by him, he merited deposition—should be written down in the form of articles, to be publicly read and declared to the people. . . . And immediately, as it appeared from the foregoing [actions] and their result that the kingship of England, together with its appurtenances, was vacant, the aforesaid Henry, duke of Lancaster, rising from his place and standing so erect that he could be well seen by all the people, humbly signing himself on the brow and breast with the symbol of the Cross and first invoking Christ by name, laid claim to the said kingship of England, thus declared vacant, together with the crown and all its members and appurtenances; [and this he did] in his mother tongue by the form of words following:

'In the name of Fadir, Son, and Holy Gost, I, Henry of Lancaster challenge this rewme of Yngland and the corone with all the membres and the appurtenances, als I that am disendit be right lyne of the blode comyng fro the gude lorde Kyng Henry Therde, and thorghe that ryght that God of his grace hath sent me, with the helpe of my kyn and of my frendes, to recover it—the whiche rewme was in poynt to be undone for defaut of governance and undoyng of the gode lawes.'

After which declaration and claim the lords both spiritual and temporal, and all the estates there present, were asked singly and in common what they thought of that declaration and claim; and the same estates, together with all the people, unanimously agreed without difficulty or delay that the aforesaid duke should reign over them. And immediately . . . the aforesaid archbishop, taking the said King Henry by the right hand, led him to the royal throne aforesaid. And after the said king, kneeling before the said throne, had made a short prayer, the same archbishop of Canterbury, with the assistance of the aforesaid archbishop of York, placed the said king and caused him to sit on the aforesaid royal throne, while the people in their excessive joy loudly applauded. And then the said archbishop of Canterbury, when silence had with difficulty been obtained, on account of the joy of all the bystanders, preached a brief sermon. . . . And when this sermon had been ended, the said Lord King Henry, in order to put at rest the minds of his subjects, in the same place publicly spoke the following words:

'Sires, I thank God and yowe, spiritual and temporal and all the estates of the lond, and do yowe to wyte[1] it is noght my will that no many thynk that be waye of conquest I wold disherit any man of his heritage, franches, or other ryghtes that hym aght to have, no put hym out of that that he has and has had by the gude laws and customs of the rewme—except thos persons that has ben agan the gude purpose and the commune profyt of the rewme.'

❖

Franciscan Sympathy for Richard II
(1402)

Source: '*Eulogium Historiarum*', trans. D. W. Whitfield, *Franciscan Studies XVII* (1957), quoted E. F. Jacob, *The Fifteenth Century* (1961), pp. 28–9

The King   [Henry IV] . . . Did you say that King Richard is alive?

Frisby   I do not say that he is alive, but I do say that if he is alive he is the true King of England.

The King   He abdicated.

Frisby   He did abdicate; but under compulsion while in prison, and that is not a valid abdication.

1. Would have you know.

The King	He abdicated right willingly.
Frisby	He would never have resigned had be been at liberty. And a resignation made in prison is not a free resignation.
The King	Even so, he was deposed.
Frisby	While he was king, he was captured by force of arms, thrown into prison, and despoiled of his realm, while you usurped his crown.
The King	I did not usurp the crown, but was duly elected.
Frisby	An election is null and void while the legitimate possessor is alive. And if he is dead you killed him. And if you are the cause of his death, you forfeit all title and any right which you may have to the kingdom.
The King	By this head of mine, thou shalt lose thine!

❧

The Royal Accounts of Henry V (1421)

Source: Proceedings of the Privy Council, ed. H. Nicolas (1834–7), Vol. II pp. 312–13, trans. Stephenson/Marcham, *op. cit.*, pp. 281–2

Sum of all the custom, subsidy, and revenue, aforesaid, £55,743 10s 10d; out of which the following expenditures must be made for annual upkeep, to wit:

For guarding the kingdom of England, annually 8000 m[arks].

Item, for Calais and the march of the same in wartime, £19,119 5s 10d.

Item, for guarding the east march and the west march of Scotland, together with Roxburgh Castle in wartime, £19,500.

Item, for guarding the land of Ireland, 2500m.

Item, for guarding Fronsac Castle, 100m.

Item, for the fees of the treasurer, the keeper of the privy seal, the justices of both benches, the barons of the exchequer, and other officials of the king's court, £3002 17s 6d.

Item, to the collectors and comptrollers of the king's customs and subsidies in the various ports of England, for their annual rewards enjoyed by virtue of their offices and received at the exchequer, £547.

Item, to divers dukes, earls, knights, and squires, to the abbess of Shene, and to divers other persons for their annuities enjoyed yearly and received at the exchequer, £722 12s 7½d.

Item, to divers persons for their annuities yearly enjoyed from divers customs in the various ports of England, £4374 4s 3d.

Item, for the fees of the collectors and comptrollers of customs in the various ports of England yearly allocated to them at the exchequer on account of their offices, £274 3s 4d.

Sum of the total annual obligation, £52,235 16s 10½d. And so the sum of the aforesaid income exceeds the aforesaid obligation [by] £3700 13s 11¾d. From which amount provision must be made [for the following needs] to wit:

For the chamber of the king and queen.

Item, for the household of the king and the queen.

Item, for the wardrobe of the king and the queen.

Item, for the king's works.

Item, for the construction of a new tower at Portsmouth.

Item, for the office of clerk of the king's ships.

Item, for keeping the king's lions and the fee of the constable of the Tower of London.

Item, for artillery and divers other matters ordained for the king's wars.

Item, for the custody and support of the king's prisoners.

Item, for the king's embassies.

Item, for divers messengers, parchments, and other expenses and necessities.

Item, for the expenses of the duchess of Holland.

And no provision has as yet been made [for the following matters] to wit:

For the old debts of the city of Harfleur.

Item, for the old debts of the city of Calais.

Item, for the old debts of the king's wardrobe.

Item, for the old debts of the king's household.

Item, for the old debts pertaining to the office of clerk of the king's ships.

Item, for the old debts pertaining to the office of clerk of the king's works.

Item, for arrears of annual fees.

Item, for executing the will of King Henry IV with regard to the debts of the same king.

Item, for the debts of the king [Henry V] while he was prince.

✦

The Minority of Henry VI

Source: Rotuli Parliamentorum (1767), Vol. IV p. 174, trans. G. B. Adams and H. M. Stephens, *op. cit.*

Be it remembered that on the twenty-seventh day of this parliament, the tender state of our most revered king Henry the Sixth after the conquest was considered, that he himself cannot personally decide in these days in respect to the protection and defence of his English realm and English church. The said lord king, fully confident of the prudence and diligence of his very dear uncles, John duke of Bedford, and Humphrey duke of Gloucester, and with the assent and advice of the lords spiritual and temporal, in the present parliament, and also with the assent of the commons of the English realm in the same parliament, has ordained and appointed his said uncle, duke of Bedford, now in foreign parts, protector and defender of his realm and the aforesaid English church and chief counsellor of his lord the king and that the duke shall be made and nominated protector and defender of his realm and chief counsellor of the king himself after he shall have returned to England and shall have come into the presence of the aforesaid lord the king and from that time as long as he shall remain in the said realm and as long as it shall be pleasing to our said lord the king. And further, our lord the king, with the aforesaid assent and advice, has ordained and appointed in the absence of his aforesaid uncle the duke of Bedford, his aforesaid uncle the duke of Gloucester now in his realm of England, protector and defender of his realm and the English church and chief counsellor of the said lord the king; and that the same duke of Gloucester be made and nominated protector and defender of the said English realm and church and chief counsellor of the said lord the king as long as it shall be pleasing to the king. . . .

✦

The Ambition of Humphrey, Duke of Gloucester (1427)

Source: op. cit., Vol. IV pp. 326–34, trans. C. Stephenson and F. G. Marcham, pp. 267–8

. . . It is to be remembered that, on March 3 of the present year, the illustrious prince, my lord Humphrey, duke of Gloucester . . . immediately after the opening of the same parliament, among other matters, declared that he, in the absence of the illustrious prince, my lord John, duke of Bedford, his dearest brother, acted as protector and defender of the kingdom of England and chief councillor of the lord king [Henry VI], and that, through the relation of certain persons, he had heard there were divers opinions concerning his authority and power. The aforesaid duke of Gloucester, therefore desirous of being more fully informed in this matter of his power and authority, particularly urged and requested all the lords spiritual and temporal assembled in the present parliament that they, through the good discretion and advisement of all, would discuss and consider such power and authority of his and with all possible speed give him sure information in that matter, stating that he would absent himself from the chamber of the parliament aforesaid until response should be made to him in this connection. When this declaration and request had been heard . . . all and singular of the lords spiritual and temporal had a certain response drawn up in writing and put into an indenture, which afterwards . . . was delivered to the aforesaid duke of Gloucester by the venerable father, Henry, archbishop of Canterbury; of which response the tenor follows in these words:

High and mighty prince, my lord of Gloucester, we, lords spiritual and temporal assembled by command of the king our sovereign lord in this his present parliament, well remember how . . ., in the first parliament held at Westminster by our sovereign lord the king who now is, you desired to have the government of this land, affirming that it belonged to you of right, as well as by virtue of your birth as by the last will of the late king, your brother [Henry V]—whom God assoil! . . . Whereupon the lords spiritual and temporal then assembled in parliament . . . held great and long deliberation and advisement, sought precedents in the government of the land for similar times and cases when kings of this land had been of tender age, also obtained information concerning the laws of the land from such persons as were notably learned therein, and finally found your said desire unjustified and groundless according to precedent and the law of the land, which the late king during his lifetime could not alter, change, or abrogate by his last will or otherwise without the consent of the three estates, nor could he consent or grant to any person the government or rule of this land for a longer term than that of his own life. . . . Nevertheless, to preserve peace and tranquillity, and in order to ease and appease you, it was ordained and established by the authority of the king with the assent of the three estates of this land that, in the absence of my lord your brother of Bedford, you should be chief of the king's council; and accordingly a title was devised for you different from that of the other councillors—not the title tutor, lieutenant, governor, or regent, nor any title that would imply authority of government over the land, but the title of protector and defender, which implies a personal duty of attending to the actual defence of the land, as well against outward enemies, if the case requires, as against inward rebels, should there be any—which God forbid! And therewith you were granted certain power, which is specified and contained in an act of the said parliament, to continue as long as might be the king's pleasure. And if the intent of the said estates had been for you to have more power or authority, more would have been expressed therein. . . . With all our hearts we marvel that, considering the open declaration of the authority and power belonging to my lord Bedford, to you in his absence, and to the king's council, to which [declaration] both my lord of Bedford aforesaid and you purely and simply subscribed, you should in any way be stirred or moved not to content yourself therewith, or to lay claim to any other. . . . Accordingly, considering the facts and causes aforesaid and many others too long for enumeration, we, the lords aforesaid, pray, exhort, and require you to content yourself with the power set forth and declared above . . . and that you neither desire nor exercise any larger power; giving you, as our answer to your aforesaid demand, that which is above written, and which without variance or change we will keep and abide by. . . .

✦

Henry VI

Source: The Great Chronicle, ed. C. L. Kingsford (1905), p. 212

And thus was this ghostly and virtuous prince Henry the Sixth . . . restored unto his Right and Regality of the which he took no great rejoice in pride, but meekly thanked God, and gave all his mind to serve and please him, and followed little or nothing of the pomp or vanities of this world, wherefore after my mind he might say as Christ said to Pilate, *Regnum meum non est de hoc mundo,* for God had endowed him with such grace that he chose with Mary

Magdalene the life contemplative, and refusal of Martha the active, the which he forsook not from his tender age unto the last day of his life, howbeit that he had many occasions to the contrary.

✦

Edward IV

i. Source: Sir Thomas More, *History of King Richard III*, ed. P. Kendall (1965) pp. 31–3

This noble prince deceased at his Palace of Westminster and, with great funeral honour and heaviness of his people from thence conveyed, was interred at Windsor—a king of such governance and behaviour in time of peace (for in war each party must needs be other's enemy) that there was never any prince of this land attaining the crown by battle so heartily beloved by the substance of the people, nor he himself so specially in any part or his life as at the time of his death. This favour and affection, even after his decease— by the cruelty, mischief and trouble of the tempestuous world that followed increased more highly towards him. At such time as he died, the displeasure of those that bore him grudge for the sake of King Henry the Sixth, whom he deposed, was well assuaged and in effect quenched, in that many of them were dead in more than twenty years of his reign—a great part of a long life—and many of them in the mean season had grown into his favour, of which he was never strange.

He was a goodly personage and very princely to behold: of heart courageous, politic in counsel, in adversity nothing abashed, in prosperity joyful rather than proud, in peace just and merciful, in war sharp and fierce, in the field bold and hardy, and nevertheless no further than wisdom would, adventurous. Whoso well consider his wars, shall no less commend his wisdom where he withdrew than his manhood where he vanquished. He was of visage lovely;

of body mighty, strong and clean made; howbeit in his latter days, with over liberal diet, somewhat corpulent and burly but nevertheless not uncomely. He was in youth greatly given to fleshly wantonness, from which health of body in great prosperity and fortune, without a special grace, hardly refrains. This fault not greatly grieved the people, for no one man's pleasure could stretch and extend to the displeasure of very many, and it was without violence; over that, in his latter days, it lessened and was well left.

In which time of his latter days this realm was in quiet and prosperous estate: no fear of outward enemies; no war in hand, nor none towards but such as no man looked for; the people towards the Prince, not in a constrained fear, but in a willing and loving obedience; among themselves, the commons in good peace. The lords whom he knew at variance, himself in his death-bed appeased. He had left off all gathering of money (which is the only thing that withdraws the hearts of Englishmen from a Prince), nor anything intended he to take in hand by which he should be driven thereto, for his tribute out of France he had before obtained, and the year foregoing his death he had obtained Berwick. And albeit that all the time of his reign he was with his people so benign, courteous, and so familiar that no part of his virtues was more esteemed, yet that condition in the end of his days (when many princes, by a long-continued sovereignty, decline into a proud port from the debonair behaviour of their beginning) marvellously in him grew and increased. This was so far true that in the summer, the last that he ever saw, his Highness, being at Windsor hunting, sent for the Mayor and Aldermen of London for none other errand but to have them hunt and be merry with him. There he made them not so stately but so friendly and so familiar cheer, and sent them venison from thence so freely into the city, that no one thing, in many days before, got him either more hearts or more hearty favour among the common people, who oftentimes more esteem and take for greater kindness a little courtesy than a great benefit.

So deceased (as I have said) this noble knight in that time in which his life was most desired ....

ii. *Source:* Commines, *Memoires,* quoted J. J. Bagley, *Historical Interpretation* (1965), p. 202

King Edward was not a person of any great management or fore-sight, but he was invincibly courageous, and the most handsome prince my eyes ever beheld.

❖

iii. *Source: op. cit.,* p. 212

Louis XI on Edward IV (1475)

He is a very handsome prince, a great admirer of the ladies. Who knows but that some of them may appear to him so charming that they will give him a desire to make us a second visit. His prede-cessors have already been too often in Paris and Normandy, and I do not care for his company so near. But on the other side of the water I shall esteem him my friend and good brother....

❖

Warwick the Kingmaker

i. *Source: op. cit.,* p. 202

This earl of Warwick, because of the outstanding service he had given him and the care he had taken of his education, might well have been called King Edward's father. Indeed, he was a very great man; for, as well as his patrimony, he held several large estates which the king had given him, some of them crown lands and some that had been appropriated. He was made governor of Calais, and had other important offices, so that, according to what I have heard, he received annually in pensions and that kind of reward 80,000 crowns, besides his inheritance.

ii. *Source:* Sir Thomas More, *History of King Richard III*, ed. P. Kendall (1965), pp. 85–6

The same Earl was a wise man and a courageous warrior and of such strength, what with his lands, his allies, and favour with all the people, that he made kings and put down kings almost at his pleasure—and it were not impossible for him to have attained it [the throne] himself if he had not reckoned it a greater thing to make a king than to be a king. But nothing lasts always; for in conclusion King Edward returned, and, with much less number, at Barnet on the Easter Day field slew the Earl of Warwick with many other great lords of that party.

◆

Sir John Fortescue's Advice on the King's Council

Source: The Governance of England, ed. C. Plummer (1885), pp. 349–51

It is thought good that it should please the king to establish a council of twelve spiritual and twelve temporal men, of the most wise and indifferent that can be chosen in all the land. And that there shall be chosen to them yearly four lords spiritual and four lords temporal, or in less number. And that the king do no great thing touching the rule of his realm, nor give land, fee, office or benefice, but that first his intent be communed and disputed in that council, and that he have heard their advices thereupon, which may in no-thing restrain his power, liberty or prerogative. And then shall the king not be counselled by men of his chamber, of his household, nor other which cannot counsel him; but the public good shall by wise men be conducted to the prosperity and honour of the land, to the surety and welfare of the king, and to the surety of all them that be about his person, whom the people have often times slain for the miscounselling of their Sovereign lord. But the aforesaid twenty-four councillors may take no fee, clothing nor rewards, or be in any man's service, otherwise than as the Justices of the law may do. Many other articles need to be added hereto which were now too long to be remembered herein. Nevertheless it is thought that the great officers, as Chancellor, Treasurer, and Privy Seal, the Judges, Barons of the Exchequer and the Clerk of the Rolls may be of this Council when they will come thereto, or when the said twenty-four and eight lords will desire them to be with them.

And for as much as it may be thought that the establishment of such a council shall be a new and great charge to the king, it is to be considered, how that the old council in England, which was mostly of great lords, that more attended to their own matters than to the universal good, and therefore procured themselves to be of the council, was more of a great charge to the king than this council shall be, and nothing of such profit. For this council shall almost continually study and labour upon the good politic weal of the land, as to provide that the money be not borne out of the realm, and how bullion may be brought in, how merchandisers and commodities of the land may keep their prices and value, how foreigners cast not down the price of the commodities growing in the land, and such other points of policy. And also how the law may be formally kept, and reformed thereas it is defective, to the greatest good and surety of the wealth of the land that hath been seen in any land. And truly there hath been given in late days to some one lord temporal much more livelihood in yearly value than will pay the wages of all the new council. And also the spiritual men of this new council shall not need to have so great wages as the temporal men which when they come to the council must leave in their countries a household for their wives, children and servants, or else carry them with them, which the spiritual men need not to do.

The Lack of Order

NORFOLK

Source: Paston Letters, quoted J. J. Bagley, *Historical Interpretation* (1965), p. 191

Right worshipful husband, I recommend me to you, and pray you to get some crossbows, and windlasses to bend them with, and bolts; for your house here be so low that there may no man shoot out with no long bow, though we had never so much need. I suppose you could have such things of Sir John Fastolf if you would send to him. And also I would you could get two or three short poleaxes to keep doors with, and also many jackets if you may.

Partrich and his fellowship are sore afeared that you would enter back upon them, and they have made great ordnance within the house, as it is told me. They have made bars to bar the doors crosswise, and they have made wickets on every quarter of the house to shoot out at, both with bows and hand-guns; and those holes that be made for hand-guns, they be scarce knee high from the floor; and of such holes be made five. There can be no man shoot out at them with no hand bows. . . .

DEVON

Source: Nicholas Radford, G. H. Radford, trans. of the Devonshire Association, Vol. XXXV (1903), pp. 265–8, quoted J. R. Lander, *The Wars of the Roses* (1965), pp. 82–4

The Thursday the 23rd day of October the year of your noble reign 38th [1455] Sir Nicholas Radford was in God's peace and yours in his own place called Uppecote in the town of Cadley in the same shire [Devon]. There came the same day and year Thomas Courtenay, late of Tiverton in the same shire, knight, son to

Thomas, Earl of Devonshire . . . with other riotous persons . . . arrayed in manner of war and, greatly against the peace of you, sovereign lord, at midnight of the same Thursday, the same place assaulted and beset it all about. The said Nicholas, his wife, and all his meinie, at that time being there in their beds. The which misdoers as soon as they had beset the said place they made there a great shout and the gates of the said place set a-fire. And the said Nicholas Radford awoke, and hearing a great noise and stirring about his said place, arose and opened the window of his chamber. And he seeing the said gates on fire asked what they were that were there, and whether there were any gentlemen among them. And Nicholas Philippe answered and said, 'Here is Sir Thomas Courtenay.'

And then the said Sir Thomas Courtenay hearing the said Nicholas Radford speak called to him, saying in this wise, 'Come down Radford and speak with me.' And then the said Nicholas Radford knowing the voice . . . answered . . . 'Sir, and ye will promise me on your faith and truth, and as ye are true knight and gentleman, that I shall have no bodily harm, no hurt of my goods, I will come down to you.' And then the said Sir Thomas Courtenay answered . . . 'Radford, come ye to me, and I promise you as I am true knight and gentleman ye shall be safe both of your body and of your goods.' Whereupon the said Nicholas Radford trusting faithfully upon that promise . . . did set open the gates and let him in . . . And the said Nicholas seeing so much people within his said place was sore afeared, and said . . . 'Sir, what do all these people here?' and he answered again and said 'Radford, ye shall have none harm' . . . And there the said Sir Thomas subtly held the said Nicholas with tales while the said Sir Thomas' men brake up the chamber doors and coffers of the said Nicholas, and then and there the misdoers . . . the said Nicholas of £300 and more in money numbered, being in his trussing coffers, and other goods and jewels, bedding, gowns, furs, books and ornaments of his chapel to the value of 1,000 marks and more, feloniously robbed, and the goods they trussed together, and with the said Nicholas Radford's own horse, carried them away.

And among other rifling then and there they found the said Nicholas Radford's wife in her bed, sore sick as she hath been this two year and more, and rolled her out of her bed, and took away the sheets that she lay in, and trussed them with the remnant of the said goods.

And after that the said Sir Thomas left his talking with the said Nicholas . . . and said . . . 'Have do Radford, for thou must go with me to my lord my father' . . . And he went forth with him a stone's cast . . . and there the said Sir Thomas communed privily with the said Nicholas Philippe . . . and rode his way and said 'Farewell Radford'. And the said Nicholas Philippe . . . him then and there feloniously and horribly slew and murdered . . . And forthwith after the said horrible murder and felony thus done, the said Sir Thomas Courtenay with all the said misdoers rode to Tiverton . . . where the said earl . . . feloniously recetted, comforted and harboured them.

✦

The Battle of Barnet (1471)

Source: Paston Letters ed. J. Fenn (1924), Vol. II pp. 102–5, letter 311

Mother, I recommend me to you, letting you know, that blessed be God, my brother John [Paston] is alive and fareth well, and in no peril of death, nevertheless he is hurt with an arrow on his right arm beneath the elbow; and I have sent him a surgeon, which hath dressed him, and he telleth me that he trusteth that he shall be all whole within right short time.

It is so that John Mylsent is dead, God have mercy on his soul! and William Mylsent is alive, and his other servants all be escaped by all likelihood.

Item, as for me, I am in good case, blessed be God; and in no jeopardy of my life as me list myself; for I am at my liberty if need be.

Item, my lord archbishop is in the Tower; nevertheless I trust to

God that he shall do well enough; he hath a safeguard for him and me both; nevertheless we have been troubled since, but now I understand that he hath a pardon; and so we hope well.

There are killed upon the field, half a mile from Barnet, on Easter day, the Earl of Warwick, the Marquis Montagu, Sir William Tyrrell, Sir Lewis Johns, and divers other esquires of our country, Godmerston and Booth.

And on the King Edward's party, the Lord Cromwell, the Lord Say, Sir Humphrey Bourchier of our country, which is a sore mourned man here; and other people of both parties in the number of more than a thousand.

As for other things, [it] is understood here, that the Queen Margaret is verily landed and her son in the west country, and I trow that as to-morrow, or else the next day, the King Edward will depart from hence to her ward to drive her out again.

Item, I beseech you that I may be recommended to my cousin Lomner, and to thank him for his good will to me ward if I had had need, as I understood by the bearer thereof; and I beseech you on my behalf to advise him to be well ware of his dealing or language as yet, for the world I assure you is right queasy, as ye shall know within this month; the people here feareth it sore.

God hath showed himself marvellously like him that made all, and can undo again when he list; and I can think that by all likelihood shall show himself as marvellous again, and that in short time; and as I suppose oftener than once in cases like.

Item, it is so that my brother is unprovided of money, I have helpen him to my power and above; therefore, as it pleaseth you, remember, for [I] cannot purvey for myself in the same case.

Written at London the Thursday in Easter week.

❖

Benevolences (1483)

Source: Statutes of the Realm (1810–28), Vol. II p. 478, trans. C. Stephenson and F. G. Marcham, *op. cit.*, p. 278

... our lord the king, remembering how the commons of this his realm, through new and unlawful inventions and inordinate avarice, against the law of the realm have been subjected to great servitude and unbearable charges and exactions, and especially so through a new imposition called benevolence, whereby in divers years the subjects and commons of this land have, against their will and freedom, paid great sums of money to their almost complete ruin— for many and divers honourable men of this realm were on that account compelled of necessity to break up their households and to live in great penury and wretchedness, with their debts unpaid and their children unpreferred, and such memorials as they had ordered for their souls' health were set at naught, to the great displeasure of God and the destruction of this realm—therefore wills and or-dains by the advice and consent of his said lords and commons in the said parliament assembled, and by the authority of the same, that henceforth his subjects and the commonalty of this his realm shall in no way be burdened with any such charge or imposition called benevolence, or anything like it; and that such exactions called benevolences as before this time have been taken shall not be held as a precedent for placing such or similar charges upon any of his said subjects of this realm in the future, but that they are to be condemned and annulled forever.

Richard III

Source: Sir Thomas More, *History of Richard III*, ed. P. Kendall (1965), pp. 35–6, 143

Richard, the third son, of whom we now treat, was in wit and courage equal with either of them, in body and probity far under them both: little of stature, ill-featured of limbs, crook-backed, his left shoulder much higher than his right, hard-favoured of visage and such as is in princes called warlike, in other men otherwise. He was malicious, wrathful, envious, and, from before his birth, ever froward. It is for truth reported that the Duchess his mother had so much ado in her travail that she could not be delivered of him uncut, and that he came into the world with the feet forward—as men be borne out of it—and (as the fame runs) also not untoothed: either men out of hatred report above the truth or else nature changed her course in his beginning who in the course of his life many things unnaturally committed. No evil captain was he in the war, as to which his disposition was more meet than for peace. Sundry victories had he and sometimes overthrows, but never for any lack in his own person, either of hardiness or politic order. Free was he called of spending and somewhat above his power liberal: with large gifts he got him unsteadfast friendship, for which he was fain to pillage and spoil in other places, and get him steadfast hatred.

He was close and secret, a deep dissembler, lowly of countenance, arrogant of heart, outwardly companionable where he inwardly hated, not hesitating to kiss whom he thought to kill, pitiless and cruel, not for evil will always but oftener for ambition and either for the surety or increase of his position. 'Friend' and 'foe' were to him indifferent: where his advantage grew, he spared no man's death whose life withstood his purpose. He slew with his own hands—as men constantly say—King Henry the Sixth, being prisoner in the Tower, and that without commandment or knowledge of the King, who would undoubtedly, if he had intended that thing, have appointed that butcherly office to some other than his own born brother.

Some wise men also think that his drift, covertly conveyed, lacked not in helping forth his brother of Clarence to his death, which he resisted openly, howbeit somewhat (as men deemed) more faintly than he that were heartily minded to his welfare. . . .

He reigned two years, one month, and twenty-seven days. He was but of a small stature, having but a deformed body, the one shoulder was higher than the other; he had a short face and a cruel look, which did betoken malice, guile, and deceit. And while he did muse upon anything, standing, he would bite his underlip continually, whereby a man might perceive his cruel nature; within his wretched body, he strived and chaffed always within himself; also the dagger which he bore about him, he would always be chopping of it in and out. He had a sharp and pregnant wit, subtle, and to dissimulate and feign very meet. He had also a proud and cruel mind, which never went from him to the hour of his death, which he had rather suffer by the cruel sword, though all his company forsake him, than by shameful flight favour his life, which after might chance by sickness or other condign punishment shortly to perish.

✦

The Landing of Henry of Richmond (1485)

Source: Paston Letters, ed. J. Fenn (1924), Vol. II p. 242, letter 443

To my well-beloved friend John Paston, be this bill delivered in haste.

Well-beloved friend, I commend me to you; letting you to understand that the king's enemies be a-land, and that the king would have set forth as upon Monday, but only for our Lady-day, but for certain he goeth forward as upon Tuesday, for a servant of mine brought to me the certainty.

Wherefore I pray you that you meet with me at Bury, for, by the grace of God, I purpose to lie at Bury as upon Tuesday night; and that ye bring with you such company of tall men as ye may goodly make at my cost and charge, besides that which ye have promised the king; and I pray you, ordain them jackets of my livery, and I shall content you at your meeting with me.

Your lover,
J. Norfolk.

◆

The Battle of Bosworth (1485)

Source: Polydore Vergil, *English History*, ed. Sir H. Ellis (1844), pp. 226–7

The report is that king Richard might have sowght to save himself by flight; for they who wer abowt him, seing the soldiers even from the first stroke to lyft up ther weapons febly and fayntlye, and soome of them to depart the feild pryvyly, suspectyd treason, and exhorted him to flye, yea and whan the matter began manyfestly to qwaile, they browght him swyft horses; but he, who was not ignorant that the people hatyd him, owt of hope to have any better hap afterward, ys sayd to have answeryd, that that very day he wold make end ether of warre or lyfe, suche great fearcenesse and such huge force of mynd he had: wherfor, knowinge certanely that that day wold ether yeald him a peaceable and quyet realme from hencefurth or els perpetually bereve him the same, he came to the fielde with the crowne uppon his head that herby he might ether make a beginning or ende of his raigne. And so the myserable man had suddenly suche end as wont ys to happen to them that have right and law both of God and man in lyke estimation, as well, impyeties, and wickednes. Surely these are more vehement examples by muche than ys hable to be utteryd with toong to tereyfy those men which suffer no time to passe free from soome haynous offence, creweltie, or mischief.

Henry, after the victory obtaynyd, gave furthwith thanks unto Almightie God for the same: than after, replenyssyd with joy incredible, he got himself unto the next hill, wher, after he had commandyd his soldiers, and commandyd to cure the woundyd, and to bury them that wer slane, he gave unto the nobylyte and gentlemen immortal thanks, promysing that he wold be myndfull of ther benyfyttes, all which meane whyle the soldiers cryed, God save king Henry, God save king Henry! and with hart and hand utteryd all the shew of joy that might be; which whan Thomas Stanley dyd see, he set anon king Richerds crowne, which was fownd among the spoyle in the feilde, uppon his head, as thoughe he had bene already by commandment of the people proclamyd king after the maner of hys auncestors, and that was the first signe of prosperytie. After that, commanding to pak upp all bag and baggage, Henry with his victorious army procedyd in the evening to Leycester, wher, for refresshing of soldiers from ther travaile and panes, and to prepare for going to London, he taryed two days. In the meane time the body of king Richard nakyd of all clothing, and layd uppon an horse bake with the armes and legges hanginge downe on both sydes, was browght to thabbay of monks Franciscanes at Leycester, a myserable spectacle in good sooth, but not unwoorthy for the mans lyfe, and there was buryed two days after without any pompe or solemne funerall. He raigned two yeres and so many monethes and one day over. He was lyttle of stature, deformyd of body, thone showlder being higher than thother, a short and sower cowntenance, which seemyd to savor of mischief, and utter evydently craft and deceyt. The whyle he was thinking of any matter, he did contynually byte his nether lyppe, as thowgh that crewell nature of his did so rage agaynst yt self in that lytle carkase. Also he was woont to be ever with his right hand pulling out of the sheath to the myddest, and putting in agane, the dagger which he did alway were. Truly he had a shap witt, provydent and subtyle, apt both to counterfayt and dissemble; his corage also hault and fearce, which faylyd him not in the very death, which, whan his men forsooke

69

him, he rather yealded to take with the swoord than by fowle flyght to prolong his lyfe, uncertane what death perchance soon after by sicknes or other vyolence to suffer.

✦

Henry VII

Source: Polydore Vergil, *English History*, quoted J. J. Bagley, *Historical Interpretation* (1965), pp. 237–8

His body was slender but well built and strong; his height above average. His appearance was remarkably attractive and his face was cheerful, especially when speaking; his eyes were small and blue, his teeth few, poor and blackish; his hair was thin and white; his complexion sallow. His spirit was distinguished, wise and prudent: his mind was brave and resolute and never, even at moments of the greatest danger, deserted him. He had a most pertinacious memory. Withal he was not devoid of scholarship. In government he was shrewd and prudent, so that no one dared to get the better of him through deceit or guile. He was gracious and kind and was as attentive to his visitors as he was easy of access. His hospitality was splendidly generous; he was fond of having foreigners at his court and he freely conferred favours on them. But those of his subjects who were indebted to him and who did not pay him due honour or who were generous only with promises, he treated with harsh severity. . . .

✦

The Hundred Years War

1. THE BATTLE OF CRÉCY (1346)

Source: The Chronicles of Jean le Bel, trans. and ed. P. E. Thompson (1966), pp. 68–71

Next morning [Saturday 26 August] they left Abbeville with banners unfurled, and it was a great sight to see these lords finely dressed and nobly mounted, with pennons fluttering in the breeze— an army estimated at twenty thousand men-at-arms on horseback, and more than a hundred thousand on foot, of whom twelve thousand were pikemen or Genoese. The King of England had no more than four thousand horsemen, ten thousand archers and ten thousand Welsh and foot-soldiers.

King Philip urged his men on to follow the English, and sent a party of knights and squires to spy out where they were, for he believed they could not be far off. When they had gone four leagues they returned with the report that the English could not be more than another few leagues away. He then gave orders for a valiant and experienced knight to go ahead with few others and find out the disposition of the English forces. These brave knights gladly undertook their mission, and on their return found some of their own banners had advanced to within a league of the English; they made these halt to await the others, then they went back to the king and said they had seen the English less than a league away, drawn up in three divisions. The king therefore held a council to decide on their action, and asked this valiant knight, Le Moine de Bazeilles, to give them his opinion. He replied that he was unwilling to speak in front of the great lords, but that it was his duty to do so. 'My Lord,' he said, 'your army is widely scattered, and it will be late before it can be all assembled. I would advise you to camp for the night, and then after mass in the morning to draw up your battle array and advance on your enemy in the name of God and Saint Denis, for I am certain from what I have seen that they will not flee, but will await your coming.'

The king was pleased with this advice, and would gladly have followed it. But when he gave orders that everyone should retreat with his banner—for the English were arrayed very close to them— none would do so unless those in the van came back first, and those in the van refused to retreat because they thought it shameful to do so; meanwhile those at the rear continued to advance and thus the valiant knight's advice was wasted through the pride and envy of the lords. They still rode proudly ahead, one in front of the other without any order, and came within sight of the English, who were waiting for them in careful array, and now it was even more shameful to turn back.

Then the commanders of the pikemen and the Genoese crossbowmen ordered their men forward in front of the companies of the lords so as to shoot first at the English, and they advanced close enough to loose their arrows on the enemy. But very soon pikemen and Genoese were routed by the English archers and would have taken to flight if the companies of the chief lords had not been so fired with envy of each other that they did not wait to make a concerted attack, but rushed forward in such disorder that the pikemen and the Genoese were trapped between them and the English. The weaker horses fell on top of them, and the others trampled them and fell on top of each other like a litter of piglets. The arrows of the English were directed with such marvellous skill at the horsemen that their mounts refused to advance a step; some leapt backwards stung to madness, some reared hideously, some turned their rear quarters towards the enemy, others merely let themselves fall to the ground and their riders could do nothing about it. The English lords, who were on foot, advanced among them striking at their will, because they could not help themselves on their horses.

The misfortunes of the French lasted until midnight, for it was nearly dark when the battle began, and the King of France and his company never came near to the fighting. At the end it was necessary for the king to withdraw from where he was, and Comte Jean de Hainault, who had been detailed as the king's personal bodyguard, took his bridle, conducted him sadly and unwillingly from the field, and rode with him through the night to Labroye, where the king took some rest, very sick at heart. Next day he continued to Amiens to await those that remained of his men. This sorry remnant of the French—lords, knights and others—who were left behind, withdrew like routed men, uncertain where to go, for it was pitch dark, not knowing of any town or village, and not having eaten all day. They went off in groups of three or four like lost men, and did not know whether their leaders or brothers or cousins were dead or had escaped. Never did a greater disaster befall any christian men than happened then to King Philip and his army. . . .

I have recorded the truth as exactly as I could, as I heard it from the mouth of my lord and friend Comte Jean de Hainault, whom may God absolve, and from ten or a dozen knights of his household, who were in the thick of the fight with the valiant and noble King of Bohemia, and who had their horses killed under them. I have also heard similar accounts from several knights of England and Germany who were engaged on the other side.

2. THE BATTLE OF AGINCOURT (1415)

Source: Jean de Waurin, '*Receueil des Chroniques et Anchiennes Istories de la Grant Bretaigne, à repsent nommé Engleterre*', ed. W. Hardy and E. L. C. P. Hardy (1868), Vol. I pp. 210–13

Of the mortal battle of Azincourt, in which the King of England discomfited the French.

It is true that the French had arranged their battalions between two small thickets, one lying close to Azincourt, and the other to Tramecourt. The place was narrow, and very advantageous for the English, and, on the contrary, very ruinous for the French, for the said French had been all night on horseback, and it rained, and the pages, grooms, and others, in leading about the horses, had broken up the ground, which was so soft that the horses could with difficulty step out of the soil. And also the said French were so loaded with armour that they could not support themselves or move forward. In the first place they were armed with long coats of steel, reaching to the knees or lower, and very heavy, over the leg harness; wherefore this weight of armour, with the softness of the wet ground, as has been said, kept them as if immovable, so that they could raise their clubs only with great difficulty, and with all these mischiefs there was this, that most of them were troubled with hunger and want of sleep. There was a marvellous number of banners, and it was ordered that some of them should be furled. Also it was settled among the said French that everyone should shorten his lance, in order that they might be stiffer when it came to fighting at close quarters. They had archers and cross-bowmen enough, but they would not let them shoot, for the plain was so narrow that there was no room except for the men-at-arms.

Now let us return to the English. After the parley between the two armies was finished, as we have said, and the delegates had returned, each to their own people, the King of England, who had appointed a knight called Sir Thomas Erpingham to place his archers in front in two wings, trusted entirely to him, and Sir Thomas, to do his part, exhorted every one to do well in the name of the king, begging them to fight vigorously against the French in order to secure and save their own lives. And thus the knight, who rode with two others only in front of the battalion, seeing that the hour was come, for all things were well arranged, threw up a baton which he held in his hand, saying 'now strike', which was the signal for attack; then dismounted and joined the king, who was also on foot in the midst of his men, with his banner before him. Then the English, seeing this signal, began suddenly to march, uttering a very loud cry, which greatly surprised the French. And when the English saw that the French did not approach them, they marched dashingly towards them in very fine order, and again raised a loud cry as they stopped to take breath.

Then the English archers, who, as I have said, were in the wings, saw that they were near enough, and began to send their arrows on the French with great vigour. The said archers were for the most part in their doublets, without armour, their stockings rolled up to their knees, and having hatchets and battle-axes or great swords hanging at their girdles; some were bare-footed and bare-headed, others had caps of boiled leather, and other of osier, covered with harpoy [skins] or leather.

Then the French, seeing the English come towards them in this fashion, placed themselves in order, every one under his banner, their helmets on their heads. The constable, the marshal, the admirals, and the other princes earnestly exhorted their men to fight the English well and bravely; and when it came to the approach the trumpets and clarions resounded everywhere; but the French began to hold down their heads, especially those who had no bucklers, for the impetuosity of the English arrows, which fell so heavily that no one durst uncover or look up. Thus they went forward a little, then made a little retreat, but before they could come to close quarters, many of the French were disabled and wounded by the arrows; and when they came quite up to the English, they were, as has been said, so closely pressed one against another that none of them could lift their arms to strike against their enemies, except some that were in front, and these fiercely pricked with the lances which they had shortened to be more stiff, and to get nearer their enemies.

The company under Sir Clugnet de Brabant who were detailed to break the line of the English archers were reduced from eight hundred to seven score before the attempt was made. Sir Guillaume de Saveuses, who was also in this company, rushed ahead of his own men, thinking they would follow him, but before he had dealt many blows among the archers he was pulled from his horse and killed. Most of the others and all their horses were driven back among the vanguard by fear of the English archers, and there they did much damage, breaking the line in several places; so many of the horses were wounded by the English arrows that their riders could not control them, and they caused many more knights to fall and so disordered their ranks that some fled behind the enemy in fear of their lives, and others were forced to withdraw into some newly-sown land. Their example caused many more French from the main body to flee.

As soon as the English saw this disorder in the vanguard they all entered the fray, and throwing down bows and arrows, they took their swords, axes, mallets, billhooks and staves and struck out at the French, many of whom they killed, until they came up with the main army. The King of England and his bodyguard followed close behind the archers. . . . As they advanced they killed cruelly and without mercy; if a man who was down could be got on his feet by his servant he might escape, because the English were so single-mindedly killing and taking prisoners as they advanced that they had no time to pursue those who fled. When all the rearguard, who had remained on horseback, saw the first two divisions getting the worst of it, they all took to flight with the exception of some of their leaders.

❖

The Agincourt Song

Source: Medieval Carols, ed. J. Stevens (1952) p. 6

Our king went forth to Normandy
With grace and might of chivalry;
There God for him wrought marvellously
Wherefore England may call and cry
Deo gracias.

He set a siege, forsooth to say,
To Harflu town with royal array;
That town he won and made affray
That France shall rue till Domesday:
Deo gracias.

Then went him forth our king comely;
In Agincourt field he fought manly;
Through grace of God most marvellously
He had both field and victory:
Deo gracias.

There lordës, earlës and baron
Were slain and taken and that soon,
And some were brought into London
With joy and bliss and great renown:
Deo gracias.

Almighty God he kept our king,
His people and all his well-willing,
And give them grace withouten ending;
Then may we call and safely sing:
Deo gracias.

❖

Livery and Maintenance (1390)

Source: Statutes of the Realm (1810–28), Vol. II p. 74, trans. C. Stephenson and F. G. Marcham, *op. cit.*, pp. 243–4

Whereas by the laws and customs of our realm, which we are bound, by the oath made at our coronation, to preserve, all our lieges within the same realm, as well poor as rich, ought freely to sue, defend, receive and have justice and right, and the accomplishment and execution thereof, in any our courts whatsoever and elsewhere, without being disturbed or oppressed by maintenance, menace, or in any other manner; and now so it is, that in many of our parliaments heretofore holden, and namely, in the parliaments last holden at Cambridge and Westminster, grievous complaint and great clamour hath been made unto us, as well by the lords spiritual and temporal as by the commons of our said realm, of great and outrageous oppressions and maintenances made to the damage of us and of our people, in divers parts of the same realm, by divers maintainors, instigators, barrators, procurors, and embraceors of quarrels and inquests in the country, whereof many are the more encouraged and hold in their maintenance and evil deeds aforesaid, because that they be of the retinue of lords and others of our said realm, with fees, robes, and other liveries, called liveries of company. We have ordained and straitly forbidden, by the advice of our great council, that no prelate, nor other man of holy Church, nor bachelor, nor esquire, nor other of less estate, give any manner of such livery called livery of company, and that no duke, earl, baron, or banneret give such livery of company to knight or esquire, if he be not retained with him for the term of his life for peace and for war, by indenture, with fraud or evil device, or unless he be a domestic and familiar abiding in his household; nor to any valet called yeoman archer, nor to other of less estate than esquire, if he be not, in like manner, a familiar abiding in his household. And that all lords spiritual and temporal, and all others of what condition or estate they be, shall utterly oust all such maintainors, instigators, barrators, procurors, and embraceors of quarrels and inquests from their fees, robes, and all manner of liveries and from their service, company, and retainer, without receiving any such on their retainer, in any manner, in time to come; and that no lord spiritual nor temporal, nor any other, that hath or shall have people of his retinue, shall suffer any that belong to him, to be a maintainor, instigator, barrator, procuror, or embraceor of quarrels and inquests in the country, in any manner, but shall put them away from his service and retinue, as afore is said, as soon as it can be discovered; and that if any lord do oust any such maintainor, instigator, barrator, procuror, or embraceor from his company for this cause, that then no other lord do retain or receive him of his retinue nor of his company in any manner, and that none of our lieges, great nor small, of what condition or estate he be, whether he be of the retinue of any lord, or other person whatever who belongeth not to any retinue, shall not undertake any quarrel other than his own, nor shall maintain it, by himself nor by other, privily nor openly; and that all those who use and wear such livery of company, contrary to this our ordinance, shall leave them off altogether within ten days after the proclamation of this same ordinance, without using or wearing them any more afterwards, and that this our ordinance be held and firmly kept, and duly executed, in all points, as well by those who have or shall have people of their retinue, as by all other persons, in that which to them belongeth touching the same ordinance, upon pain of imprisonment, fine and ransom, or of being punished in other manner, according as shall be advised by us and our council: wherefore we command and charge you that incontinently, upon sight hereof, you cause to be published and proclaimed this our ordinance in cities, boroughs, market towns, and other public places, within your bailiwick, as well within franchise as without, and do cause the same to be holden and duly executed in all points.

Given under our great seal at Westminster, the twelfth day of May.

By the king himself and the council.

❖

Indentures

1. EDWARD III AND HENRY HUSEE (22 MARCH 1347)

Source: Historical Interpretation, J. J. Bagley (1965), p. 148

This indenture, made between our lord Edward king of England and of France and lord of Ireland of the one part and Henry Husee of the other part, witnesses that the said Henry has undertaken the defence of the Isle of Wight until next Michaelmas with forty men-at-arms and sixty archers at the king's expense. He will begin to be responsible for these same men and for the island immediately after Easter, and he will be paid wages for the said men at a rate agreed between himself and the treasurer of our lord the king.

In witness of this, our said lord the king holds the part of this indenture concerning the said Henry, and the said Henry holds the other part of the same indenture concerning our said lord the king. And they have attached their seals.

Given at Westminster the 22 day of March, the year of the reign of our said lord the king, namely, of England the twenty-first and of France the eighth.

2. JOHN OF GAUNT AND SIR ROGER TRUMPINGTON
(29 August 1372)

Source: op. cit., pp. 175–6

... our lord has granted the said Roger for life, for himself and a squire, forty marks a year in English coinage in time of peace, to be taken from the revenues of the manors of Glatton and Holm in the county of Huntingdon, and to be paid by the lord's receiver at Michaelmas and Easter in equal portions. Both in peace and war the said Sir Roger will be required to serve our said lord, and to go with him to war wherever he wishes, with a squire suitably and well equipped. And each year he will take his fees of war, as stated above, for himself and his squire, together with such wages as are paid to others of his rank. And the said Sir Roger shall begin his year of war on the day he sets out from home to join our said lord in accordance with instructions which will be sent to him, and thus he shall be entitled to wages for himself and his squire for reasonable travelling time going and returning. And the said Sir Roger shall provide such adequate equipment for himself, his men and horses as can be reasonably expected. As for war-horses taken and lost in our lord's service, and as for prisoners or other prizes taken or won by the said Sir Roger or his esquire or one of his servants, our lord will recompense him as he will recompense others of his rank.

3. LORD HASTINGS AND NICHOLAS AGARDE
(28 APRIL 1474)

Source: Lord Hastings' Indentured Retainers, 1461–83, W. H. Dunham
(1955), p. 126

This indenture made the XXVIII day of April the XIV year of
the reign of our sovereign lord, King Edward the IV, between
William, Lord Hastings, on the one part and Nicholas Agarde, gentle
man, on the other part, witnesseth that the said Nicholas of his own
desire and motion is belaft and retained for the term of his life with
the foresaid Lord Hastings afore all other, to ride and go with the
same lord and him assist, aid and his part take against all other
persons within the realm of England. The liegance and faith which
he oweth to our said sovereign lord the king and to my lord prince
and to their heirs only except. And the said Nicholas at all times shall
come to the said Lord Hastings upon reasonable warning, accompanied with as many persons defensibly arrayed as he may goodly
make or assemble, at the cost and expenses of the same lord. For the
which the same lord promiseth to be a good and tender lord to the
said Nicholas in all thing reasonable that he hath to do, and him to
aid and succour in his right as far as law and conscience requireth.
In witness whereof the foresaid parties to these present indentures
interchangeably have set their seals and signs manual. Given this
day and year aforesaid.

Nicholas Agarde

English Fleets and Shipping

1. A LEVY OF SHIPS (1227)

Source: Close Rolls (1833–44), Vol. II p. 211, trans. C. Stephenson and F. G. Marcham, *op. cit.*, p. 137

The king to the bailiffs and good men of Dunwich, greeting. Know that, by the counsel of our faithful men, we are making preparations, God willing, to cross the sea in our own person. Wherefore we command and firmly enjoin you that, in the fealty by which you are bound to us, you have all good ships of your port, besides those you owe us through your promise, come to Portsmouth well equipped and supplied with arms and victuals; so that at the latest they shall be there on the approaching feast of St. James the Apostle, in the eleventh year of our reign, ready to cross the sea with our body.

By witness of the king, at Westminster.

2. NAVAL LEVIES (1242)

Source: Close Rolls 1237–42 (1902), p. 456, trans. C. Stephenson and F. G. Marcham, *op. cit.*, p. 40

The king to the barons of Hastings, greeting. Whereas, on account of his continuous injuries we are under no obligation to observe a truce toward the king of France, and whereas war between us has already broken out: we have decided, by your aid and counsel and by that of our other barons of the Cinque Ports, to assail the said king and his men both by sea and by land and to fight him in every way we can. Therefore, especially relying on your manliness and faith for willing and powerful aid in this affair, we command and urge you, in the fealty by which you are bound to us and as you cherish us and our honour, that as quickly as possible you have your ships prepared and well manned; and that, together with our other barons of the Cinque Ports, to whom we have sent the same mandate, you equip yourselves for assailing the said king of France along the coasts of Brittany, Normandy, and Boulogne, both by sea and by land, with fire and with other weapons at your command; yet so that you, on account of this our mandate, shall not presume to cause damage or injury to churches, or to any one who enjoys our protection or safe conduct—saving also to us the fifth which, as you know, belongs to us from booty acquired by you in our wars. . . . In testimony whereof, etc., to continue during our pleasure. By witness of the king, at Xanten, June 8.

3. SERVICE FROM THE CINQUE PORTS (1293)

Source: Red Book of the Exchequer (1896), Vol. II p. 714, trans. C. Stephenson and F. G. Marcham, *op. cit.*, pp. 162–3

It is to be remembered that, on the octave of St. Hilary in the twenty-first year of King Edward, son of King Henry, when Stephen of Penchester, then constable of Dover [Castle] and warden of the Cinque Ports, in connection with his account for his aforesaid bailiwick was present in the exchequer before Master William de la Marche, the treasurer, and the barons of the same exchequer, and after the said Stephen had been interrogated at length concerning the aforesaid Cinque Ports—namely, as to which were the ports and which their members, and as to what services the said ports owed the king, and how and in what way [they were owed]—the same Stephen informed the aforesaid treasurer and barons to this effect:

Sussex. Hastings is a chief port, the members of which are these: Winchelsea, Rye, the lathe of Pevensey, and Bulverhythe in the county of Sussex; Bekesbourne and Grange in the county of Kent. Which port, with its aforesaid members, ought on the king's summons to find twenty-one ships; and in each ship there ought to be twenty-one men, strong, fit, well-armed, and prepared for the king's service; but so that, on the king's behalf, summons should thereof be made forty days before. And when the aforesaid ships and the men in them have come to the place whither they have been summoned, they shall there remain in the king's service for fifteen days at their own cost. And if the king needs their service beyond the fifteen days aforesaid, or wishes them to remain there longer, those ships with the men in them shall remain in the king's service so long as he pleases and at his cost: that is to say, a master shall receive 6d. per day, a constable 6d. per day, and each of the others 3d. per day.

Kent. Romney is the chief port, and Old Romney and Lydd are members of the same. Which port, with its members, shall find five ships for the king in the manner aforesaid. The port of Hythe owes the king five ships in the manner aforesaid. Dover is a chief port, the members of which are these: Faversham, Folkestone, and Margate. This port, with its aforesaid members, owes twenty-one ships in the manner aforesaid. Sandwich is a chief port, the members of which are Fordwich, Stonor, and Sarre. Which port, with its members, owes the king five ships in the manner aforesaid.

Total service of the Cinque ports, fifty-seven ships.

4. ORDINANCE FOR THE USE OF ENGLISH SHIPS (1382)

Source: Statutes of the Realm (1810–28), Vol. II p. 17, trans. C. Stephenson and F. G. Marcham, *op. cit.*, p. 238

... to increase the navy of England, which is now greatly diminished: it is assented and accorded, that none of the king's liege people do from henceforth ship any merchandise in going out or coming within the realm of England, anywhere, but only in ships of the king's liegeance; and every person of the said liegeance, which ... do ship any merchandise in any other ships ... shall forfeit to the king all his merchandises shipped in other vessels, wheresoever they be found hereafter, or the value of the same. ...

Source: op. cit., Vol. II p. 502, trans. C. Stephenson and F. G. Marcham, p. 300

Item, in the said parliament it was called remembrance of the great minishing and decay that hath been now of late time of the navy within this realm of England, and idleness of the mariners within the same, by which this whole realm within short process of time, without reformation be had therein, shall not be of habilite and power to defend itself: wherefore at the prayer of the said commons, the king our sovereign lord, by the advice of the lords spiritual and temporal, in this said present parliament assembled, and by authority of the same, it is enacted, ordained and established, that no manner of person of what degree or condition that he be of, buy nor sell within this said realm, Ireland, Wales, Calais or the marches thereof, or Berwick, from the feast of Michaelmas next now coming, any manner of wines of the growing of the duchy of Guyenne or of Gascony, but such as shall be aventured and brought in an English, Irish or Welshman's ship or ships, and the mariners of the same English, Irish or Welshmen for the more part, or men of Calais or of the marches of the same; and that upon pain of forfeiture of the same wines so bought or sold contrary to this act, the one half of that forfeiture to be to the king our sovereign lord and that other half to the finder of that forfeiture: this act and ordinance to endure betwixt this and the next parliament, saving alway to the king his prerogative.

❖

The Ordinance of the Staple (1353)

Source: op. cit., Vol. I p. 332, trans. Stephenson/Marcham, pp. 228–30

Edward by the grace of God king of England and of France, and lord of Ireland, to all our sheriffs, mayors, bailiffs, ministers, and other our faithful people to whom these present letters shall come, Greeting: Whereas, good deliberation had with the prelates, dukes, earls, barons and knights of the counties, that is to say of every county, one for all the county, and of the commons of cities and boroughs of our realm of England, summoned to our great council, holden at Westminster the Monday next after the feast of Saint Matthew the apostle, the seven and twentieth year of our reign of England, and of France the fourteenth, for the damage which hath notoriously come as well to us and to the great men, as to our people of our realm of England, and of our lands of Wales and Ireland, because that the staple of wools, leather and woolfells of our said realm and lands have been holden out of our said realm and lands, and also for the great profits which should come to the said realm and lands if the staple were holden within the same, and not elsewhere; to the honour of God, and in relief of our realm and lands aforesaid and for to eschew the perils that may happen of the contrary in time to come, by the counsel and common assent of the said prelates, dukes, earls, and barons, knights and commons aforesaid, we have ordained and established the things underwritten, that is to say:

1. First, that the staple of wools, leather, woolfells, and lead, growing or coming forth within our said realm and lands, shall be perpetually holden at the places underwritten, that is to say, for England at Newcastle-upon-Tyne, York, Lincoln, Norwich, Westminster, Canterbury, Chichester, Winchester, Exeter, and Bristol; for Wales, at Carmaerthen, and for Ireland, at Dublin, Waterford, Cork, and Drogheda, and not elsewhere: and that all the said wools, as well old as new, woolfells, leather and lead, which shall be carried out of the said realm and lands, shall be first brought to the said

staples, and there the said wool and lead, betwixt merchant and merchant, or merchant and others, shall be lawfully weighed by the standard; and that every sack and sarpler of the same wools so weighed, be sealed under the seal of the mayor of the staple; and that all the wools so weighed and sealed at the staple of York, Lincoln, Norwich, Westminster, Canterbury and Winchester, and also leather, woolfells, and lead which shall come there, the customs of the staple thereof paid, shall be witnessed by bill, sealed with the seal of the mayor of the staple, and brought to the ports under-written, that is to say, from York to Hull, from Lincoln to Saint Botolf, from Norwich to Great Yarmouth, from Westminster to London, from Canterbury to Sandwich, and from Winchester to Southampton; and there the said wools and lead shall be another time weighed by our customers assigned in the same ports; and all the wool and lead brought to the said ports of Newcastle, Chichester, Exeter, Bristol, Carmaerthen, Dublin, Waterford, Cork and Drogheda, where the other staples be holden, shall be but once weighed by the standard betwixt merchant and merchant, or merchant and other, in presence of our customers there; and an indenture shall be made betwixt the mayor of the staple being in the port of the sea, and our customers there, of all the wools and lead so weighed, and also of all the leather and woolfells which shall come to the said staples to pass there; and the same wools and lead, and also the leather and woolfells customed and cocketed, and the customs thereof duly paid to our said customers in all these said ports, that is to say, of denizens for the time that they have passed, half a mark of a sack of wool, half a mark of three hundred woolfells, a mark of a last of leather, and of aliens ten shillings of a sack of wool, ten shillings of three hundred woolfells, and twenty shillings of a last of leather, and three pence of every twenty shillings of lead, then the said merchandises shall be carried by merchants strangers which have bought the same, and not by Englishmen, Welshmen, nor Irishmen, to the parts beyond the sea out of the said realm and lands, to what parts it shall please the said merchants strangers: and that the said mayor and customers shall delay no man willingly for gain; not for such cause, nor in other manner, shall any take of any person to do that which pertaineth to their office, upon pain of imprisonment, and to pay the party the double of that which they have so taken, and also of that which the party shall be endamaged because of such taking or delay, and moreover be ransomed at our will, but shall hold them content of that which they did take in certain to do their office: and that the mayor of the staple and customers take an oath of all the merchants which so shall pass with wools, leather, woolfells and lead that they shall hold no staple beyond the sea, of the same merchandises.

2. Item, ... we have ordained and established, that all merchants strangers, which be not of our enmity, of what land or nation that they be, may safely and surely under our protection and safe-conduct come and dwell in our said realm and lands where they will, and from thence return with their ships, wares and all manner of merchandises, and freely sell their merchandises at the staple and elsewhere within the same realm and lands, to any that will buy them, paying the customs thereof due. ...

❖

Parliamentary Institutions and Procedures

1. THE FIRST PARLIAMENT OF SIMON DE MONTFORT (1264)

Source: W. Stubbs, *Select Charters* (1913), p. 399, trans. C. Stephenson and F. G. Marcham, *op. cit.*, p. 150

The king to Adam of Newmarket, greeting. Whereas the disturbance recently experienced in our kingdom has now subsided and, by the grace of divine co-operation, peace has now been ordained and established between us and our barons; and [whereas] in order that this peace may be inviolably observed throughout our entire kingdom, it has been provided by the counsel and assent of our barons that in each of our counties throughout England keepers of our peace shall be appointed for the defence and security of those parts, until other provision for the state of our kingdom may be made by us and our barons; and whereas, relying on your fidelity as well as your industry, we, by the counsel of our said barons, have assigned you as our keeper in the county of Lincoln during our pleasure: we command and firmly enjoin that, in the fealty by which you are bound to us, you there diligently see to the keeping of our peace and to those matters which pertain to it, as aforesaid. . . . And whereas in our approaching parliament, it is necessary for us to deliberate with our prelates, magnates, and other faithful men concerning our affairs and those of our kingdom: we command you to send to us on behalf of the entire county aforesaid four of the more lawful and discreet knights of the same county elected for that purpose by the assent of that county; so that they shall be with us at London on the octave of the approaching feast of the Holy Trinity at the latest, in order to deliberate with us on the aforesaid affairs. . . . By witness of the king at St. Paul's in London, June 4.

2. SUMMONS OF REPRESENTATION OF SHIRES AND TOWNS TO PARLIAMENT (1298)

Source: Source Book of English History, ed. G. C. Lee (1900), p. 183

The king to the sheriff of Northamptonshire. Since we intend to have a consultation and meeting with the earls, barons and other principal men of our kingdom with regard to providing remedies against the dangers which are in these days threatening the same kingdom; and on that account have commanded them to be with us on the Lord's day next after the feast of St. Martin in the approaching winter, at Westminster, to consider, ordain, and do as may be necessary for the avoidance of these dangers, we strictly require you to cause two knights from the aforesaid county, two citizens from each city in the same county, and two burgesses from each borough, of those who are especially discreet and capable of labouring, to be elected without delay, and to cause them to come to us at the aforesaid time and place.

Moreover, the said knights are to have full and sufficient power for themselves and for the community of the aforesaid county, and the said citizens and burgesses for themselves and the communities of the aforesaid cities and boroughs separately, then and there for doing what shall then be ordained according to the common counsel in the premises; so that the aforesaid business shall not remain unfinished in any way for defect of this power. And you shall have there the names of the knights, citizens and burgesses and this writ.

Witness the king at Canterbury on the third day of October.

3. PARLIAMENTARY CONTROL OF DIRECT TAXATION (1340)

Source: Statutes of the Realm (1810–28), Vol. I pp. 289–91, trans. C. Stephenson and F. G. Marcham, *op. cit.*, p. 223

. . . Whereas the prelates, earls, barons, and commons of our realm, in our present parliament summoned at Westminster . . . of their free will and grace have granted us, in aid of advancing the great enterprises that we have before us both on this side of the sea and beyond it, the ninth sheaf, the ninth fleece, and the ninth lamb . . . and [whereas] the citizens of cities and the burgesses of boroughs [have granted] the true ninth of all their goods; and [whereas] foreign merchants and other men who live neither from trade nor from flocks of sheep, [have granted] the fifteenth of their goods, rightly [assessed] according to value: we, desirous of providing indemnity for the said prelates, earls, barons, and others of the said commonalty, and also for the citizens, burgesses, and merchants, that this grant now chargeable shall not at another time be treated as a precedent or work to their prejudice in the future; and that henceforth they shall be neither charged nor burdened to make common aid or to sustain charge except by the common assent of the prelates, earls, and barons, and of the other lords and commons of our said realm of England, and this in parliament; and that all profits arising from the said aid, and from wardships, marriages, customs, and escheats, together with other profits arising from the kingdom of England, shall be devoted and spent to maintain the safeguarding of our said kingdom of England and [to advance] our wars in Scotland, France, and Gascony, and nowhere else during the said wars. . . .

And whereas the said prelates, earls, barons, and commons, for the sake of the great enterprises which we have undertaken, have granted at our request that we may levy 40s. on each sack of wool passing beyond sea from now until the feast of Pentecost next; and 40s. on every three-hundred wool-fells; and 40s. on a last of leather: we . . . have granted that, after the said feast of Pentecost to come in one year, neither we nor our heirs shall demand, assess, levy, or cause to be levied more than half a mark of custom on a sack of wool throughout all England, half a mark on three hundred wool-fells, and one mark on a last of leather. . . .

4. PARLIAMENTARY DEBATE IN 1376

Source: Anonimalle Chronicle, ed. V. H. Galbraith (1927), pp. 80–2, trans. C. Stephenson and F. G. Marcham, op. cit., pp. 220–2

. . . And on the said second day all the knights and commons aforesaid assembled and went into the chapter house and seated themselves about [the room] one next another. And, they began to talk about their business, the matters before the parliament, saying that it would be well at the outset for them to be sworn to each other to keep counsel regarding what was spoken and decided among them, and loyally and without concealment to deliberate and ordain for the benefit of the kingdom. And to do this all unanimously agreed, and they took a good oath to be loyal to each other. Then one of them said that, if any of us knew of anything to say for the benefit of the king and the kingdom, it would be well for him to set forth among us what he knew and then, one after the other, [each of the rest could say] what lay next his heart.

Thereupon a knight of the south country rose and went to the reading desk in the centre of the chapter house so that all might hear and, pounding on the said desk, began to speak in this fashion: '*Jube domine benedicere*, etc.[1] My lord, you have heard the grievous matters before the parliament—how our lord the king has asked of the clergy and the commons a tenth and a fifteenth and customs on wool and other merchandise for a year or two. And in my opinion it is much to grant, for the commons are so weakened and impoverished by the divers tallages and taxes which they have paid up to the present that they cannot sustain such a charge or at this time pay it. Besides, all we have given to the war for a long time we have lost because it has been badly wasted and falsely expended. And so it would be well to consider how our lord the king can live and govern his kingdom and maintain the war from his demesne property, and not hold to ransom his liegemen of the land. Also, as I have heard, there are divers people who, without his knowledge, have in their hands goods and treasure of our lord the king amounting to a great sum of gold and silver; and they have falsely concealed the said goods, which through guile and extortion they have gained in many ways to the great damage of our lord the king and the kingdom. For the present I will say no more. *Tu autem domine miserere nostris.*' And he went back to his seat among his companions.

Thereupon another knight arose and went to the reading desk and said: 'My lords, our companion has spoken to good purpose, and now, as God will give me grace, I will tell you one thing for the benefit of the kingdom. You have heard how it was ordained by common counsel in parliament that the staple of wool and other merchandise should be wholly at Calais, to the great advantage of our lord the king; and then the said town was governed and ruled by merchants of England, and they took nothing by way of payments to maintain the war or for the government of the said town. And afterwards the said staple was suddenly removed to divers cities and towns of England, and the merchants were ousted from Calais, together with their wives and their households, without the knowledge or consent of parliament, but for the benefit of a few, illegally and against the statute thereupon made; so that the lord of Latimer and Richard Lyons of London and others could have advantages.

1. He begins and ends his speech with a conventional Latin grace.

And by concealment they took great sums of the maltote, which rightfully the king should have, because each year, to keep the town, the king spends sums amounting to £8000 of gold and silver, without getting anything there, where no expense used to be necessary. Wherefore it would be well to provide a remedy by advising that the staple should be restored to Calais.' And he would say no more, but went back to his seat.

And the third man rose and went to the reading desk and said: 'My lords, our companions have spoken very well and to good purpose. But it is my opinion that it would not be profitable or honourable for us to deliberate on such great affairs and such grievous matters for the benefit of the kingdom without the counsel and aid of those greater and wiser than we are, or to begin such procedure without the assent of the lords. Wherefore it would be well at the outset to pray our lord the king and his wise council in the parliament that they may grant and assign to us certain bishops and certain earls, barons, and bannerets, such as we may name, to counsel and aid us and to hear and witness what we shall say.' And to this all agreed. Then two or three more arose in the same manner, one after the other, and spoke on various subjects. . . .

About the same time a knight from the march of Wales, who was steward to the earl of March and was named Sir Peter de la Mare, began to speak where the others had spoken, and he said: 'My lord, you have well heard what our companions have had to say and what they have known and how they have expressed their views; and, in my opinion, they have spoken loyally and to good purpose.' And he rehearsed, word for word, all the things that they had said, doing so very skilfully and in good form. And besides he advised them on many points and particulars, as will be more fully set forth below. And so they ended the second day.

Then on the third day all the knights and commons assembled in the said chapter house and day after day until the next Friday held discussion concerning various matters and [particularly] the extortions committed by divers persons, through treachery, as they were advised. During which discussion and counsel, because the said Sir Peter de la Mare had spoken so well and had so skilfully rehearsed the arguments and views of his companions, and had informed them of much that they did not know, they begged him on their part to assume the duty of expressing their will in the great parliament before the said lords, as to what they had decided to do and say according to their conscience. And the said Sir Peter, out of reverence to God and his good companions and for the benefit of the kingdom, assumed that duty. . . .

5. LIMITATION OF THE FRANCHISE IN 1429

Source: Statutes of the Realm (1810–28), Vol. II p. 243, trans. C. Stephenson and F. G. Marcham, *op. cit.*, p. 276

. . . whereas in many counties the elections of knights of the shires, those chosen to attend the king's parliaments, have of late been carried out by too great and excessive a number of people dwelling within those same counties, of whom the larger part have been people of little substance or of no worth, each pretending to have the same voice in such elections as the most worthy knights or squires dwelling in the same counties, whereby homicides, riots, assaults, and feuds are very likely to arise among the gentlefolk and other people of the same counties unless a suitable remedy is provided in this connection; [therefore] our lord the king considering the premises, has provided and ordained by the authority of this parliament that knights of the shires, elected to attend parliaments hereafter to be held in the kingdom of England, shall be chosen in each county by persons dwelling and resident therein, each of whom shall have a freehold to the value of at least 40s. a year beyond the charges . . .; and that every sheriff of England shall, by the aforesaid authority, have power to examine on the Holy Gospels each such elector, how much he is able to spend annually. . . .

The Process of Justice

1. EXTRACTS FROM THE CORONER'S ROLL OF 1266–7

Source: Select Cases from Coroners' Rolls, ed. C. Gross (1896), pp. 2–6, trans. C. Stephenson and F. G. Marcham, *op. cit.,* pp. 181–2

It happened about bedtime on Sunday next before the feast of St. Bartholomew in the fiftieth year of Henry III that Henry Colburn of Barford went out of his house in Barford to drink a tankard of beer and did not return that night; but early the next morning Agnes Colburn, his mother, looked for him and found the said Henry dead. And he was wounded in the body about the heart and in the belly with seven knife-wounds, and in the head with four wounds apparently made with a pickaxe, and also in the throat and the chin and the head as far as the brain. The aforesaid Agnes at once raised the hue and cry and pursuit was made. And she finds pledges: Humphrey Quarrel and Thomas Quarrel of the same Barford.

It happened in the vill of Wilden on Wednesday next before the feast of Simon and Jude in the fiftieth year that unknown male-factors came to the house of Jordan Hull of Wilden and broke into the said house while the said Jordan was absent. And the said malefactors wounded the said Agnes, wife of the said Jordan, and killed Emma, his eight-year-old daughter. Afterwards they carried off all the goods from the house. . . . Inquest was held before Simon Read, the coroner, by four neighbouring townships . . . who said what has been reported, and that the malefactors were unknown. . . .

It happened at Eaton on Thursday next after the feast of the Apostles Peter and Paul in the fiftieth year that Reginald Stead of Eaton, reaper of John Francis, went into the meadows of Eaton to guard the meadow of his lord and, being taken with falling sickness, collapsed and died forthwith by misadventure. Alice, his wife, was the first to discover him, and she finds pledges. . . . Inquest was held before Simon Read, the coroner, by four neighbouring townships . . . who say that he died by misadventure of the aforesaid disease, and they know nothing beyond that.

2. JUSTICES OF THE PEACE (1361)

Source: Statutes of the Realm (1810–28), Vol. I p. 364, trans. C. Stephenson and F. G. Marcham, *op. cit.*, p. 230

These are the measures which our lord the king, the prelates, the lords, and the commons have ordained in this present parliament, held at Westminster on Sunday next before the feast of the Conversion of St. Paul, to be observed and publicly proclaimed throughout the kingdom, to wit:

First, that for the keeping of the peace, there shall be assigned in each county of England one lord, and with him three or four of the most worthy men of the county together with certain men skilled in the law, and they shall have power to restrain evil-doers, rioters, and all other miscreants; to pursue, arrest, capture, and chastise them according to their trespass or offence; to have them imprisoned and duly punished according to the law and custom of the kingdom, and according to what the justices may think best to do at their discretion and good advisement. Also they shall have power to inform themselves and to make inquiry concerning all those who have been pillagers and robbers in the regions beyond the sea, and who have now returned to become vagrants, refusing to work as they used to in times past; and to take and arrest all whom they can find on indictment or suspicion, and to put them in prison. . . . Also they shall have power to hear and determine, at the king's suit, all manner of felonies and trespasses committed in the same county, according to the laws and customs aforesaid. . . . And the fine to be assessed before the justices, because of trespass committed by any person, shall be just and reasonable, according to the gravity of the offence and as the causes leading to it are taken into account. . . .

Item, it is agreed that the men assigned to keep the peace shall have power to make inquiry concerning measures and also weights, according to the statute thereupon made in the twenty-fifth year of our lord the king's reign. . . .

Item, it is agreed in this present parliament that the Statute of Labourers earlier made shall stand in all its particulars, with the exception of the pecuniary penalty, in which connection it is agreed that henceforth labourers shall not be punished by fine and redemption. . . .

Item, with regard to labourers and artisans who run away from their owed services into another vill or county, it is provided that the aggrieved party shall have his suit before the justices of the peace. . . .

3. IMPROVEMENT OF JUSTICE UNDER RICHARD II

Source: Statutes of the Realm (1810–1828), Vol. II p. 36, trans. C. Stephenson and F. G. Marcham, *op. cit.*, p. 242

Item, it is agreed and established that no man of law shall henceforth be justice of assize or of common jail delivery in his own country, and that the chief justice of the common bench, among others, shall be assigned to hold assizes of this sort and to deliver jails; but with regard to the chief justice of the king's bench, let such action be taken as has been customary for the greater part of the past hundred years.

Item, . . . after the said ordinance [of Edward III] had been recited in parliament, it was agreed and established that no justice of the king's bench or of the common bench, or any baron of the exchequer, so long as he held the office of justice or baron, should henceforth take, either by himself or through others, whether openly or in secret, any robe, fief, pension, gift, or reward from anybody except the king; nor should he take any present from anybody except one of food and drink which is not of great value. And it is established that henceforth such justices and barons shall not give counsel to any one, whether great or small, in causes or concerns to which the king is a party or which in any way touch the king; and that they are not to be of counsel to any one in any case, plea, or dispute pending before themselves or in any other great court or tribunal of the king, on penalty of forfeiting office and of paying fine and ransom to the king.

THE CHURCH

❖

A Vision of England (c. 1377)

Source: William Langland, Piers the Ploughman, trans. J. F. Goodridge (1959) pp. 63–5

One summer season, when the sun was warm, I rigged myself
out in shaggy woollen clothes, as if I were a shepherd, and in the
garb of an easy-living hermit I set out to roam far and wide through
the world, hoping to hear of marvels. But on a morning in May,
among the Malvern Hills, a strange thing happened to me, as
though by magic. For I was tired out by my wanderings, and as I
lay down to rest under a broad bank by the side of a stream and
leaned over gazing into the water, it sounded so pleasant that I fell
asleep.

And I dreamt a marvellous dream. I was in a wilderness, I could
not tell where, and looking Eastwards I saw a tower high up against
the sun, and splendidly built on top of a hill; and far beneath it was
a great gulf, with a dungeon in it, surrounded by deep, dark pits,
dreadful to see. But between the tower and the gulf I saw a smooth
plain, thronged with all kinds of people, high and low together,
moving busily about their worldly affairs.

Some laboured at plowing and sowing, with no time for pleasure,
sweating to produce food for the gluttons to waste. Others spent
their lives in vanity, parading themselves in a show of fine clothes,

But many, out of love for our Lord and in the hope of Heaven, led strict lives devoted to prayer and penance—for such are the hermits and anchorites who stay in their cells, and are not forever hankering to roam about, and pamper their bodies with sensual pleasures.

Others chose to live by trade, and were much better off—for in our worldly eyes such men seem to thrive. Then there were the professional entertainers, some of whom, I think, are harmless minstrels, making an honest living by their music; but others, babblers and vulgar jesters, are true Judas' children! They invent fantastic tales about themselves, and pose as half-wits, yet they show wit enough whenever it suits them, and could easily work for a living if they had to! I will not say all that St. Paul says about them; it is enough to quote, 'He who talks filth is a servant of the Devil.'

And there were tramps and beggars hastening on their rounds, with their bellies and their packs crammed full of bread. They lived by their wits, and fought over their ale—for God knows, they go to bed glutted with food and drink, these brigands, and get up with foul language and filthy talk; and all day long, Sleep and shabby Sloth are at their heels.

And I saw pilgrims and palmers banding together to visit the shrines at Rome and Compostella. They went on their way full of clever talk, and took leave to tell fibs about it for the rest of their lives. And some I heard spinning such yarns of the shrines they had visited, you could tell by the way they talked that their tongues were more tuned to lying than telling the truth, no matter what tale they told.

Troops of hermits with their hooked staves were on their way to Walsingham, with their wenches following after. These great long lubbers, who hated work, were got up in clerical gowns to distinguish them from laymen, and paraded as hermits for the sake of an easy life.

I saw the Friars there too—all four Orders of them—preaching to the people for what they could get. In their greed for fine clothes, they interpreted the Scriptures to suit themselves and their patrons. Many of these Doctors of Divinity can dress as handsomely as they please, for as their advances, so their profits increase. And now that

Charity has gone into business, and become confessor-in-chief to wealthy lords, many strange things have happened in the last few years; unless the Friars and Holy Church mend their quarrel, the worst evil in the world will soon be upon us.

There was also a Pardoner, preaching like a priest. He produced a document covered with Bishops' seals, and claimed to have power to absolve all the people from broken fasts and vows of every kind. The ignorant folk believed him and were delighted. They came up and knelt to kiss his documents, while he, blinding them with letters of indulgence thrust in their faces, raked in their rings and jewellery with his rolled parchment!—So the people give their gold to support these gluttons, and put their trust in dirty-minded scoundrels. If the Bishop were worthy of the name, if he kept his ears open to what went on around him, his seal would not be sent out like this to deceive the people. But it is not by the Bishop's leave that this rogue preaches; for the parish priest is in league with the Pardoner, and they divide the proceeds between them—money which, but for them, would go to the poor of the parish.

Then I heard parish priests complaining to the Bishop that since the Plague their parishes were too poor to live in; so they asked permission to live in London, where they could traffic in Masses, and chime their voices to the sweet jingling of silver. Bishops and novices, Doctors of Divinity and other great divines—to whom Christ has given the charge of men's souls, and whose heads are tonsured to show that they must absolve, teach, and pray for their parishioners, and feed the poor—I saw them all living in London, even in Lent. Some took posts at Court counting the king's money, or in the Courts of Exchequer and Chancery, where they claimed his dues from the wards of the City and his right to unclaimed property. Others went into the service of lords and ladies, sitting like stewards managing household affairs—and gabbled their daily Mass and Office without devotion. Indeed, I fear that there are many whom Christ, in His great Consistory Court, will curse for ever.

❖

The Statute of Mortmain (1279)

Source: Statutes of the Realm (1810–28), Vol. I p. 50, trans. C. Stephenson and F. G. Marcham, *op. cit.*, p. 169

The king to his justices of the bench, greeting. Whereas it was formerly enacted that men of religion should not enter upon the fiefs of any persons without the consent and licence of the principal lords from whom those fiefs were immediately held; and whereas since then men of religion have nevertheless entered upon the fiefs of others as well as their own—by appropriating them, buying them, and sometimes by receiving them through gifts of other men —whereby the services which are owed from fiefs of this sort, and which were originally established for the defence of the kingdom, are wrongfully witheld and the principal lords lose their escheats: [therefore] we, seeking in this connection to provide a suitable remedy for the good of the kingdom, by the counsel of the prelates, earls, and other faithful men of our kingdom who are members of our council, have enacted, established, and ordained that no man of religion or any other whatsoever shall buy or sell lands or tenements, or under colour of donation, lease, or other title of any sort shall receive them from any one, or presume artfully and craftily to appropriate them in any way whatsoever, whereby land and tenements of this sort may somehow come into mortmain[1]—under pain of forfeiting the same [lands or tenements], . . . And so we command you to have the aforesaid statute read in your presence and henceforth strictly held and observed.

By witness of the king, at Westminster, November 25, in the seventh year of our reign.

❖

1. Literally, 'dead hand'—permanent possession by a church or other corporation.

The Second Statute of Praemunire
(1393)

Source: Statutes of the Realm (1810–28), Vol. II p. 85, trans. C. Stephenson and F. G. Marcham, *op. cit.*, p. 246

... Wherefore our said lord the king, by the assent aforesaid and at the prayer of his said commons, has ordained and established that, if any one purchases or pursues, or causes to be purchased or pursued, in the court of Rome or elsewhere, any such translations, processes, sentences of excommunication, bulls, instruments, or anything else touching our lord the king that is inimical to him, his crown, his regality, or his aforesaid kingdom, as aforesaid; or if any one brings them into the kingdom, receives them, or thereof makes notification or any other execution, either within the said kingdom or outside it; such persons, their notaries, procurators, partisans, supporters, abettors, and counsellors are to be put outside the protection of our said lord the king, and their lands, tenements, goods, and chattels are to be forfeit to our lord the king. And that, if they can be found, they are to be bodily attached and taken before the king and his council, there to respond in the cases aforesaid; or that process shall be brought against them by *praemunire facias*[1] in the manner provided by other statutes concerning provisors, and other men who, in derogation of our lord the king's regality, bring suit in the court of another.

❖

---

1. The special writ after which the statute came to be named.

Papal Provisions

POPE HONORIUS III WRITES TO ARCHBISHOP GRAY
OF YORK, 1220

Source: The English Church in the Fourteenth Century, W. A. Pantin
(1962), p. 41

Since those who faithfully serve the Apostolic See, as the head of
the universal Church, are held to give useful service as it were to all
the members, it is right that they should be honoured with suitable
benefices; lest otherwise, if they had to serve at their own cost and
were defrauded of special revenues, they might be slower to serve.
Whence is it the practice that clerks who reside at the Apostolic See
(not without many labours and expenses) have received for the
time being ecclesiastical benefices in England and other parts of the
world; and these not infrequently have striven in their time to
serve those from whom they have received their benefices so effica-
ciously, that it has been as much to the advantage of those who gave
the benefices as of those who received them.

◆

Pluralism in 1366

Source: op. cit., p. 40

And it is laid down in the sacred canons that a good and in-
dustrious and literate person can govern two or even ten Churches
better than another can govern one; and both he who resides and he
who does not reside are understood to serve the altar, so long as

they live a good life and expend well the income they derive. And I [Master Roger Otery] say also that by the custom of the English Church it was and is the used and approved custom, from time out of mind, and tolerated by the Roman Church, that the bishops and other patrons of the said realm of England can provide their well-deserving clerks with benefices, especially sinecures, up to any number, without any contradiction or offence to the Holy See.

✦

The Election of the Archbishop of Canterbury (1313)

Source: Life of Edward II, ed. N. Denholm-Young (1957), pp. 45–6

Because I made mention above of the death of the Archbishop of Canterbury, I turn now to his successor and the manner of his succession. On the death of the primate, the prior and convent of Christ Church, Canterbury, proceeded to an election, and by a unanimous vote chose Mr Thomas de Cobham, a nobleman, and a doctor of canon and civil law; who at once set out and crossed the sea to prosecute his cause. He was hindered by two circumstances. While the primate was still on his sick-bed the pope had sent his bull reserving for himself the disposition of the archbishopric and the choice of the next pontiff. Also the King of England sent to the pope, praying him that he should see fit to promote his clerk the Bishop of Worcester to the archiepiscopal see. For these reasons the archbishop-elect was frustrated, nor could the assent of the electors profit him, for at the king's instance, and, it is believed, after a large sum had passed, the lord pope granted the archbishopric and set the said bishop over the English church.

O what a difference there was between the elect and the 'preferred'! For the elect was the very flower of Kent, of noble stock; he had lectured in arts and on canon law, and was a master of theology; a man eminently fitted for the see of Canterbury. The bishop, on the other hand, had recently been a mere clerk and was scarcely literate, but he excelled in theatrical presentations, and through this obtained the king's favour. Thus he was taken into the king's household, and soon became the king's treasurer, and from the treasury became Bishop of Worcester, later Chancellor, and lo! now he is made Archbishop. Some are surprised at the man's good luck, but I rather am surprised at the lord pope, why he should reject so excellent a person, and deliberately adopt an unsuitable one, when the merits of each were clearly known to him. But My Lady Money transacts all business in the Curia. If perchance you are ignorant of the habit and customs of the Roman Curia, pay heed to this. It loves causes, law suits, quarrels, because they cannot be expedited without money; and a case once entered upon at Rome becomes almost immortal. . . .

Bogo de Clare

Source: Lanercost Chronicle, ed. J. Stevenson (1839), p. 158, quoted G. G. Coulton, *Life in the Middle Ages* (1910), Vol. I pp. 54–5

There died in London Bogo de Clare, illustrious in name but not in life, whose end, as men report, was not very honourable[1] yet accordant to his deserts, for he had held innumerable churches, and had ill governed such as Christ had bought with His trading. For he was a mere courtier, who cared not for Holy Orders but quenched the cure of souls and squandered the revenues of his churches; nor did he esteem Christ's spouse highly enough to pro-

1. Clarus, a pun.

vide the church out of her own revenues with necessary vestments untorn and undefiled; as might be proved by many profane instances, whereof I will tell one by way of example. In the honourable church of Simonburn, whereof he was rector, on the holy day of Easter, I saw, instead of a reredos over the high altar, a wattle of twigs daubed with fresh cow-dung; yet that living was valued at seven hundred marks yearly. Moreover, he was so wanton and wasteful that he gave the old queen of France for a gift a lady's chariot of unheard-of workmanship; to wit, all of ivory, both body and wheels, and all that should have been of iron was of silver even to the smallest nail, and its awning was of silk and gold even to the least cord whereby it was drawn; but the price whereof, as men say, was three pounds sterling; but the scandal was of a thousand thousand.

❖

A Thirteenth Century Curate

Source: Register of St Osmund, ed. W. H. R. Jones (1883), Vol. I, p. 304, quoted G. G. Coulton, *op. cit.* (1910), Vol. II pp. 39–40

Acts of the Chapter held by William, dean of Salisbury, at Sonning, in the year of our Lord 1222, on the Friday next before the Feast of St. Martin. . . . Vitalis, a priest, perpetual vicar of Sonning, presented the chaplain [i.e. curate] named Simon whom he has with him, and whom he lately engaged until Michaelmas. This Simon, examined as to his Orders, said that he was ordained archdeacon at Oxford by a certain Irish bishop named Albin, then suffragan to the Bishop of Lincoln, from whom also he received deacon's orders; and those of priest from Hugh [of Wells] now Bishop of Lincoln, four years past. He was examined in the Gospel of the first Sunday in Advent, and was found insufficient, and unable to understand what he read. Again he was tried in the Canon of the Mass, at the words *Te igitur, clementissime Pater, etc.* He knew not the case of *Te*, nor by what word it was governed; and when we bade him look closely which could most fittingly govern it, he replied: '*Pater*, for He governeth all things.' We asked him what *clementissime* was, and what case, and how declined, he knew not. We asked him what *clemens* was; he knew not. Moreover, the said Simon knew no difference between one antiphon and another, nor the chant of the hymns, nor even of the hymn *nocte surgentes*, nor did he know by heart aught of the service or psalter. Moreover, he said that it seemed indecent that he should be examined before the Dean, since he was already in Holy Orders. We asked him where he was when he received his priest's Orders: he answered that he had forgotten. He is amply illiterate.

❖

Two Fourteenth Century Priests

i. *Source:* Geoffrey Chaucer, *Canterbury Tales*, ed. N. Coghill (1951), pp. 38–9

> A holy-minded man of good renown
> There was, and poor, the Parson to a town,
> Yet he was rich in holy thought and work.
> He also was a learned man, a clerk,
> Who truly knew Christ's gospel and would preach it
> Devoutly to parishioners, and teach it.
> Benign and wonderfully diligent,
> And patient when adversity was sent
> (For so he proved in great adversity)
> He much disliked extorting tithe or fee,
> Nay rather he preferred beyond a doubt
> Giving to poor parishioners round about

(a) King John, funeral effigy,
    Worcester Cathedral

b) Edward III, wooden funeral
   effigy, Westminster Abbey

(a) *Above left:* Henry VI, bronze lectern, King's College, Cambridge

(b) *Above right:* Richard, Duke of York (d. 1460), stained glass, Trinity College, Cambridge

Opposite: Richard II, the earliest known painting of an English monarch, Westminster Abbey

4 (a) Richard III

(b) Lady Margaret Beaufort
(1443–1509)

5 (a) Henry VII, wooden funeral effigy, Westminster Abbey

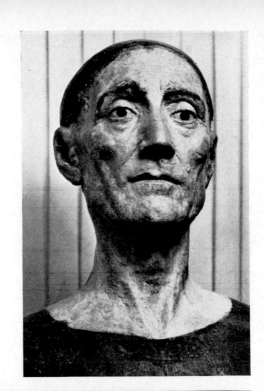

(b) Henry VII, bronze effigy by Torrigiani, Westminster Abbey

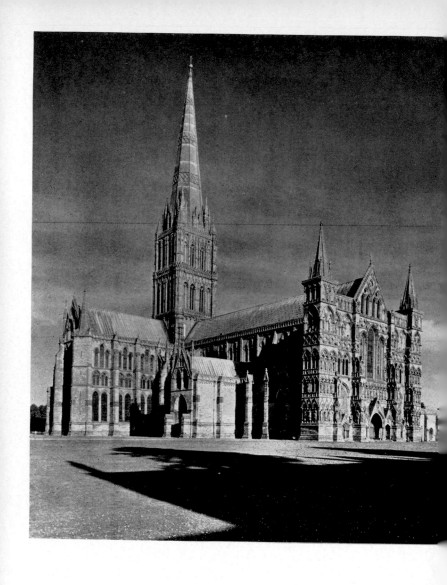

6 Salisbury Cathedral, from the north-west, 1220–c. 1250, tower mid-14th century

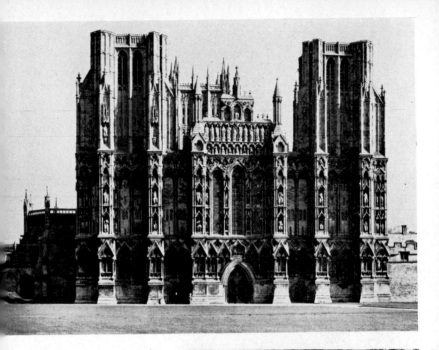

7 Wells Cathedral, c. 1225–
1250
(a) The west front

(b) The nave

9 King's College Chapel, Cambridge
(a) The main vault, looking west, 1508–1515

(b) Roof space above the main vault

10 (a) *Above:* The Church of St Peter and St Paul, Lavenham, Suffolk, 14th to 16th centuries

(b) *Below:* The Church of St Peter and St Paul, Northleach, Gloucestershire, 15th century

11 The hammer-beam roof, Church of St Wendreda,
March, Cambridgeshire, c. 1450-1500

12 (a) *Above left:* A bench-end,
c. 1500, Jesus College Chapel,
Cambridge

(b) *Above right:* The Cosmati
Pavement, marble and mosaic,
c. 1268, Westminster Abbey

13 Fountains Abbey, Yorkshire,
13th century, tower 1494–1526

14 (a) *Above:* Harlech Castle, Merionethshire, 1283–1290
(b) *Below:* Bodiam Castle, Sussex, 1386–c. 1390

15 (a) *Above:* William Grevel's house, late 14th century, Chipping Camden, Gloucestershire
(b) *Below:* Thomas Paycocke's house, c. 1500, Coggeshall, Essex

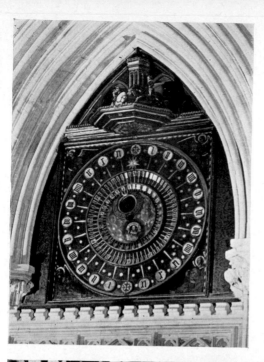

16 (a) The clock, Wells
Cathedral

(b) Chapter House doorway
Southwell Minster,
Nottinghamshire,
c. 1290–1295

7 (a) Wells Cathedral:
Capitals, south
transept. Toothache

(b) A thorn in the foot

18 The pilgrim, Lincoln Cathedral

19 The Falling Knight, misericord, Lincoln Cathedral

Est animal qd̄ dr̄ elephans· in quo n̄ est concupiscentia coit̄. Elephantem
grece a magnitudine corporis vocatū· qr̄ portitur qd̄ formidū mon
tis pferat· Grece aū mons ʒipho dr̄. Apð indos aū a voce barro vo
c̄r. Vnde e· et vox barritus· et bestia cū ebur. Rostrū aū pbosadia vl pmusada
dr̄· qr̄ illo pabula ori adhovuet· et e· ang̃u̇ similis vallo munit· eburneu. Hul
li aiāl grūdi videt· In eis cū ipse et oneri ligneis turrib̄ collocatū· omnip de muro
uactis dimicant· Intellectu et memoria multa vigent· gregatim incedunt· mure
fugiūt· auersi coeunt· Biennio aū pariunt· nec amplius qm semel gignunt·
nec plures s̄ nō vnū. Viuunt aū annos trecentos. Et dum voluerit facere filī
os· uadit ad orientē· ppe paradisū· et e· ibi arbor que vocat̄ mandragora· et va
dit cū femina sua qp̄ pr̄ accipit de arbore· et dat masc̄lo suo· et seducūt eum
dū manducat· statim̄ in utero sapit. Cū vī pariendi tempus venit exit in stagn̄
nū· et aqua venit usq̄ ad ubera matris. Elephans aū cūstodit eam parturien
tē· qr̄ dracon· e· inimic̄ elephanti· si dū inuenerit serpentē occidit eū· qr̄ guidat̄
dū mūdat̄. Est cū formidabilis pariens elephantus· cui inuit̄ inuer· si e· uadit
et si occidit n̄ potest surgere. Gladit aū cū se inclinat in arbore ut dormiat· n̄ cū
eiū iucturas grandi· Venator aū inuenit arbore mediat· cū elephans cū se
inclinauerit simul cū arbore cadat. Cadens aū clamat fortit· et statim̄ magn̄
elephans venit· et qp̄ n̄ potest cū leuare· Hunc clamāt simul et veniūt· xij· elephan
tes· et n̄ possunt cū leuare q̄ ceciderit. Deinde clamāt omn̄· et tūc venit pusillus
elephans· et mittit os suū cū pmusada subt̄ magnū elephantū· et leuat cū·

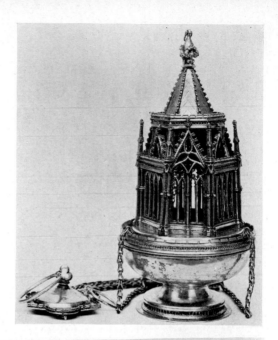

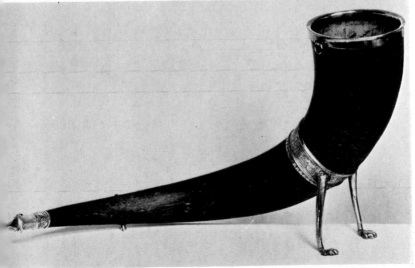

(a) *Above:* The Ramsey Abbey censer, silver-gilt, 1325–1350
(b) *Below:* A drinking horn, early 13th century

(a) *Opposite above:* A domestic brawl, misericord, Westminster Abbey
(b) *Opposite below:* An elephant, bestiary, early 13th century

Sir Roger de Trumpington, brass,
c. 1289, Trumpington,
Cambridgeshire

24 (a) *Above:* Robert de Paris and widow, brass, c. 1379, Hildersham, Cambridgeshire

(b) *Below:* Thomas and Elizabeth Camoys, brass, 1419, Trotton, Sussex

5 (a) Packhorse Bridge, Allerford,
Somerset

(b) A ship, stained glass, c. 1530,
King's College Chapel,
Cambridge

Et nos populus pascue eius: t oues
manus eius
Hodie si uocem eius audieritis: no
lite obdurare corda uestra
Sicut in irritacione: secundum diē

Preoccupemus faciem eius in con
fessione: et in psalmis iubilemus ei.
Quoniam deus magnus domi
nus: t rex magnus super omnes
deos.

26 The Luttrell Psalter, c. 1340   (a) Harrowing
                                      (b) Sowing

The Luttrell Psalter, c. 1340   (a) Reaping and binding sheaves
                                        (b) Harvest home

Se bourbon et monseigneur de
coucy car ilz ont moult fort en
tendu pour vous. Et aussi la
contesse de saint pol car la bon

Le seigneur de clary re
pondy en telle maniere et di
Grant merci a messeigneur
mais ie cuidie auoir bien fa

aff that to the knowlauge of god.

ff the departyng of this grete z hitth armee was the Sor
dan playnly enfoimed /z yn like wise the kynge of Cizile
but of all the reaume of Cizile was not one xᵗ the armi

A naval attack, Romance of the Three Kings' Sons, late 15th century

(a) *Opposite above:* Knights jousting, Froissart's Chronicle, early 15th century

(b) *Opposite below:* A tournament, Froissart's Chronicle, late 15th century

30 A royal banquet, Jean de Waurin's *Chroniques d'Angleterre*, late 15th century

32 (a) An indenture: an agreement between the Earl of Chester and Lincoln and the men of Frieston and Butterwick (1217–1232)

(b) Local reaction to the plague: inscriptions, Ashwell, Hertfordshire. The translation runs as follows:

The first pestilence was in 1350 less one
[13]49, the pestilence
1350, pitiless, wild, violent
1350, the dregs of the people live to tell the tale. At the end of the second [outbreak], a great wind
In this year [St] Maurus thunders in the heavens, 1361

NOTE The Black Death struck East Anglia in 1349. A second outbreak occurred in 1361, and was followed by the great storm of 15 January [St Maurus Day] 1361–2. The inscriptions are in verse, and it is probable that the dates which are added to the last two lines originally appeared on the worn stone to the left of those lines.

From his own goods and Easter offerings.
He found sufficiency in little things.
Wide was his parish, with houses far asunder,
Yet he neglected not in rain or thunder,
In sickness or in grief to pay a call
On the remotest whether great or small
Upon his feet, and in his hand a stave.
This noble example to his sheep he gave,
First following the word before he taught it,
And it was from the gospel he had caught it.
This little proverb he would add thereto
That if gold rust, what then will iron do?
For if a priest be foul in whom we trust
No wonder that a common man should rust;
And shame it is to see—let priests take stock—
A shitten shepherd and a snowy flock.
The true example that a priest should give
Is one of cleanness, how the sheep should live.
He did not set his benefice to hire
And leave his sheep encumbered in the mire
Or run to London to earn easy bread
By singing masses for the wealthy dead,
Or find some Brotherhood and get enrolled.
He stayed at home and watched over his fold
So that no wolf should make the sheep miscarry.
He was a shepherd and no mercenary.
Holy and virtuous he was, but then
Never contemptuous of sinful men,
Never disdainful, never too proud or fine,
But was discreet in teaching and benign.
His business was to show a fair behaviour
And draw men thus to Heaven and their Saviour,
Unless indeed a man were obstinate;
And such, whether of high or low estate,
He put to sharp rebuke to say the least.
I think there never was a better priest.
He sought no pomp or glory in his dealings,

No scrupulosity had spiced his feelings.
Christ and His Twelve Apostles and their lore
He taught, but followed it himself before.

ii. *Source: The Annals of Ghent*, ed. H. Johnstone (1951), pp. 4–5

I have heard a story about a certain goliard priest, who, when he had nothing left after consuming all his substance in feasts and drinking-bouts, stole the silver plating from a crucifix, and having sold it gave a great banquet to his cronies. Accused of this before the bishop, who summoned and severely rebuked him, he replied by these two lines:

When Guy himself had spent his pelf
He flayed his Lord to spread his board.

❖

The Arrival of the Franciscans in England (1224)

Source: Thomas of Eccleston, ed. Dr Brewer (1858), pp. 5–17, trans. and abridged G. G. Coulton, *Social Life in Britain from the Conquest to the Reformation* (1918), pp. 247–9

In the year 1224 the Friars Minor first landed in England at Dover; four clerics and five lay-brethren. . . . These nine were charitably conveyed over to England by the monks of Fécamp, and hospitably provided with all necessaries. At Canterbury, they abode two days at the Cathedral Priory; then four went forth to London, and the other five repaired to the Priests' Spital, where they abode until they had found an habitation. Soon afterwards a little room was granted unto them within the school-house. Here, from to day day, they sat almost continually enclosed; but at eventide, when the scholars were gone home, the friars came into their chamber and lit their fire and sat by the hearth. Here, when the time of Collation[1] came, they sometimes set on the fire a pot full of beer-dregs, wherein they dipped a bowl and drank all round, each saying some word of edification. And (as one hath borne witness who was of this same pure simplicity, and who was found worthy to share and partake in holy poverty) their drink was at times so thick that, when the bowl had to be warmed, they poured water in, and thus drank cheerfully. The like frequently befell them at Sarum, where the brethren so jocundly and joyfully drank their dregs round the kitchen fire at Collation, that each thought himself happy to snatch them in friendly fashion from the other. It befell also that two brethren came in great distress to one friary, when there was no beer in the house. Then the Warden, taking counsel with the elder brethren, let them borrow a gallon of beer; yet on such terms that the friars of the house, who were entertaining the guests, should make but a false show of drinking thereof, for charity's sake. Even in the London friary, I myself have seen the brethren drink beer so sour, that some preferred water; and I have seen them eat the bread called *tourte*[2] in vulgar parlance. Moreover, when there was no bread, I have for some time eaten porridge of spelt there, in the presence of the Provincial Minister and the guests.

But the four brethren aforesaid, proceeding to London, abode with the Friars Preachers, who received them kindly, and with whom they dwelt fifteen days, eating and drinking of what was set before them as most familiar guests. Then they hired for themselves a house in Cornhill, wherein they built cells, stuffing the partitions with grass. Here they dwelt in their first simplicity until the next summer, without any chapel, for as yet they had no privilege of setting up an altar and celebrating divine service. Here did the sweet Lord Jesus sow that grain of mustard-seed which afterwards became greater than all herbs. It is worthy of note that, in

1. Collation was a sup of drink and a mouthful of bread before retiring to bed.
2. A rough whole-meal bread, the roughest kind ordinarily baked; then came *bis*, then *white*, and then fancy breads such as *simnel* and *manchet*.

the thirty-second year from the advent of the Friars Minor to England, the brethren living in the English province were numbered at 1,242, in forty-nine friaries.

The first to be received was a youth of great promise, pre-eminent in bodily beauty, brother Solomon. He was wont to tell me that, while he was yet a novice, the care of the temporal things was committed unto him, and he went to beg alms at his sister's house. She, bringing him a loaf, turned away her face, and said 'Cursed be the hour that I ever set eyes on thee!' but he took the bread cheerfully and went his way. He kept so strictly to the prescribed form of extreme poverty, that he sometimes suffered so from cold as to seem on the point of death; and the brethren, having no other means of warming him, were inspired by holy charity to excogitate a pious subtlety; for they all gathered together and warmed him by pressing him to their bosom, as her litter lieth about a sow. [One day] the brethren ate at the table of the Archbishop and came home barefoot to the Canterbury friary, through snow so deep that all who saw it shuddered to see them go. After this [brother Solomon] was taken with an infirmity of one foot, whereof he lay sick in London for two years, so that he could scarcely move from place to place but if another would bear him. In this infirmity he was honoured with a visit from brother Jordan of holy memory, Master of the whole Order of Friars Preachers, who said unto him: 'Brother, be not ashamed if the Father of our Lord Jesus Christ draw thee to Himself by one foot.' When therefore he had thus lain a long while in the cellar, where he had not been able to hear mass (for the brethren sang no mass in the friary, but went to hear divine service and to sing their masses in the parish church), then his infirmity became so desperate that, as the surgeons judged, his foot must needs be cut off. But, when the axe was brought, and the foot had been bared, a little blood and matter came forth, which promised some hope; wherefore that hard judgment was deferred for a while. Meanwhile he conceived a certain hope that, if he were led to some saint, he might recover his foot and his health. Wherefore, when brother Agnello [the Provincial minister] came, he bade that brother Solomon should be taken to some shrine beyond the sea without delay, and as conveniently as might be. It came to pass, then, that his faith belied him not; nay rather, he waxed so strong as to walk without crutch, and to celebrate mass. At Cambridge, the Brethren were received first by the burghers of the town, who granted unto them the Old Synagogue, hard by the Castle. But, seeing that the neighbourhood of the prison was intolerable to them (for the gaolers and the brethren had but one door of entrance) the king gave them ten marks wherewith to buy a rent which should satisfy his exchequer for the rent of their site; and thus the brethren built a chapel so miserably poor, that a single carpenter in one day made and set up 14 pairs of rafters.

✦

Franciscans and Dominicans

i. *Source:* Matthew Paris, *English History*, ed. J. A. Giles (1852–4), Vol. I pp. 474–6

And that the world might not appear to be devoid of increasing troubles on every side, a controversy arose between the Minorite brothers [Franciscans] and Preachers [Dominicans], to the astonishment of many, because they seemed to have chosen perfection's path, viz. that of poverty and patience. On one side the Preachers declared that they were instituted first, and on that account more worthy; that they were also more decent in their apparel, and had deservedly obtained their name and office from their preaching, and that they were more truly distinguished by the apostolic dignity: on the other side, the Minorites gave answer, that they had embraced, for God, a way of living more rigorous and humble, and so the more worthy, because more holy; and that the brothers could and certainly ought to pass over from the order of Preachers to their order, as from an inferior community to one more rigorous and superior. The Preachers contradicted them to their face, saying, that though the Minorites went barefooted, coarsely clad, and girded with a rope, the privilege of eating flesh or a more delicate article of diet was not denied them even in public, a thing which is forbidden to the community of Preachers, wherefore it could not be allowed that the Preachers could enter the order of Minorites, as one more rigorous and more worthy, but quite the contrary. Therefore, between these, even as between the Templars and Hospitallers, in the Holy Land, through the enemy to the human race sowing the seeds of dissension, a great and scandalous strife arose; and inasmuch as it was between learned men and scholars, it was more dangerous to the Catholic Church, and a sign of great judgment impending at its threshold. And what is terrible, and a sad presage, for three or four hundred years, or more, the monastic order did not hasten to destruction so quickly as their order, of whom now, the brothers, twenty-four years having scarcely elapsed, had first built in England dwellings which rivalled regal palaces in height. These are they who daily expose to view their inestimable treasures, in enlarging their sumptuous edifices, and erecting lofty walls, thereby impudently transgressing the limits of their original poverty, and violating the basis of their religion, according to the prophecy of the German Hildegarde. When noblemen and rich men are at the point of death, whom they know to be possessed of great riches, they, in their love of gain, diligently urge them, to the injury and loss of the ordinary pastors, and extort confessions and hidden wills, lauding themselves and their own order only, and placing themselves before all others. So no faithful man now believes he can be saved, except he is directed by the counsels of the Preachers and Minorites. Desirous of obtaining privileges in the courts of kings and potentates, they act the parts of councillors, chamberlains, treasurers, bridegrooms, and mediators for marriages; they are the executors of the papal extortions; in their sermons they either are flatterers, or most cutting reprovers, revealers of confessions, or impudent accusers. Despising, also, the authentic orders which were instituted by the holy fathers, namely, by St. Benedict and St. Augustine, and also the followers of them (as the thing clearly appears in the case of the church of Scarborough, when the Minorites shamefully retreated), they set their own community before the rest. They look upon the Cistercian monks as clownish, harmless, half-bred, or rather ill-bred, priests; and the monks of the Black order as proud epicures.

ii. *Source: A Bill of Complaint against the Mendicant Friars delivered to the Convocation of Canterbury* (c. November 1355), quoted and trans. W. A. Pantin, *The English Church in the Fourteenth Century* (1962), pp. 159–60

... these religious, to whom the quest of beggary ought to provide a living, go about with loosened reins, flowing with delights, on noble palfreys of their own, with saddles and reins most exquisitely ornamented, beyond the manner of the greater prelates of England; they frequently visit the courts of magnates and public and prosperous places; not fearing the censures of the archbishops, bishops and other prelates of the province of Canterbury and of the English Church and of the laws and canons, they become the most biting detractors, the adulators of magnates and their confessors; they handle the secular and spiritual affairs touching our lord the King and other nobles and magnates of the land, to the prejudice of the clergy and the English church, to whom in these days they are clearly more hostile than the laity; they are astute and one-sided middlemen, corrupt and disguised under the veil of religion; they frequently even become mediators of contracts of marriage, illicitly and of their own free will, and deceitful agents of business; and by their blandishments they acquire the goodwill of the lords and ladies of the realm of England to such an extent, that very many churches in the realm of England to which they are opposed are outrageously oppressed in their legal rights; and what is more to be wept over, being the confessors of such noble lords and ladies, nay rather the betrayers and notorious deceivers of their souls, they convert to their own gain the compensation for wrong-doing which by earthly and heavenly law ought to be restored to the injured parties, and a pillow of flattery is put under the sinner's head as he sleeps in his sin; loaded with goods, they stuff their ruddy cheeks and blow out their bellies; and when they are deservedly rebuked for fomenting sin in this manner, they daily prepare intolerable plots against the English church, and secretly commit things concerning which it is not expedient to speak at present, since they hold such sway. Wherefore your clergy pray that for the salvation of the English church you would cause to be applied some timely remedy against these insolencies of the said mendicants, in this present council or by provision of the Apostolic See.

❖

The Difficulties of a Royal Abbey

Source: Cartulary of Vale Royal, Lancashire and Cheshire Record Society, Vol. 68, quoted J. J. Bagley, *Historical Interpretation* (1965), pp. 117–18

i. To our Lord the King and his council. His chaplains, the abbot and convent of Vale Royal, show that, whereas they were founded by the most honourable King Edward [I], the king's forebear, and since the time of their foundation, from year to year according as they were able, they have built a part of their church and a part of their communal house, so that by reason of the great sums spent by the convent and the bad years there have been, they must forthwith perish unless they receive some timely assistance; they therefore pray our said Lord the King, that for the love of God, as a work of charity and for the souls of his ancestors, he will be pleased of his especial grace to grant them some assistance, so that they may maintain and continue their works; which cost £37,000 from the treasury of our Lord the King, who founded the house. And whereas the aforesaid ancestor of our lord (whom God absolve from sin!) of his grace assigned to them £1,000, £490 of which are in arrears, for, from the manor of Ashford in the Peak, which was assigned to them for the same sum, they have received only £80, may it therefore please the King to continue to assign that manor to them to provide for that sum, until they shall be paid, or else the vill of Northwich in the county of Chester, or else think fit to order the chamberlain of Chester to pay that sum to the said works out of his exchequer.

ii. 1336

... in our monastery we have a very large church begun by the king of England at our first foundation [1278], but by no means finished. For at the first foundation he built it with stone walls, but the crypt remains to be built, with the roof and the glass and other ornaments of the church. Moreover, the cloister, chapter-house, dormitory, refectory and other offices of the monastery still remain to be built in a style corresponding with the church; for the accomplishment of which the rents of our house are insufficient.

◆

The Abbey of Winchcombe at the end of the Middle Ages

Source: Abbot Kidderminster, quoted David Knowles, *The Religious Orders in England* (1961), Vol. III p. 92

It was a fine sight to see how the brethren devoted themselves to sacred learning, how they made use of Latin even in their familiar conversations, and how the cloister at Winchcombe at that time had all the appearance of a young university, though on a minute scale. Added to this, their regular observance was so ardently observed among us, and brotherly charity was so honoured, that you would have said that there could not possibly be another such family, so united, so harmonious and yet so small, in the whole of England. The good God alone knows what it was then for me to be immersed in sacred studies with my brethren in the cloister. There, day and night, I passed the time at my books in a little study I had constructed; would that I had allowed it to stand till the present day!

My industry was such that practically all the learning I have in Scripture and divinity was gained there in the cloister. I have written all this that those who come after may learn that theology may be as fruitfully studied in the cloister as at the university.

❖

Lollards

Source: Henry Knighton, ed. J. R. Lumby (1889–95), trans. R. B. Morgan, *Readings in English Social History* (1923), pp. 205–9

William Smith, so called from his trade, had an insignificant and ugly person. Being crossed in love, he renounced all pleasures, and became a vegetarian and a total abstainer . . . he taught the alphabet and did clerking. Various knights used to go round protecting him from any harm for his profane teaching, for they had zeal for God but were uninstructed, for they believed what they heard from the false prophets . . . and when one of them would come to the neighbourhood of any of them to preach, they would promptly assemble the local folk with a great ado at some fixed place or church even if people did not want to but did not dare to object. . . . They would attend the sermon with sword and buckler to stop any objections to the blasphemy.

One Richard Waytestathe, priest, and this William Smith, used to have spells at St. John Baptist's chapel outside Leicester near the leper hospital. Here other sectaries met for their conventicles . . . for there was a hostelry and lodging for that kind of visitor and there they had a school of malignant doctrines and opinions and a clearing-house of heresy. The chapel had been dedicated to God but it was now an asylum for blasphemers who hated Christ's church. Once these two, Richard the priest, and William Smith, wanted a meal of herbs. They had the herbs but no fire. One peered into a corner of the chapel and saw an old image made in honour of St. Catherine, painted standing up. 'Look, dearly beloved brother,' said he, 'God has given us kindling to cook our meal. This will make a saintly fire.' So axe and flame wrought a new martyrdom, if in the heavenly kingdom the cruelty of modern torturers can make itself felt. This Lollard sect hated images and worked against them calling them idols. . . . If anyone mentioned St. Mary of Lincoln or St. Mary of Walsingham they would call them names like 'wiche of Lincolle', and 'wiche of Walsyngham'. So one took the axe and the other took the image, saying, 'Let's test if it's really a saint, for if it bleeds when we knock the head off we'll have to adore it, but if not it can feed our fire and cook our vegetables.' When they came out they could not hide their shame, but gave themselves away to their cost by boasting about it as funny. They were soon after turned out of the inn. . . .

The number of people with such beliefs multiplied fast and filled the kingdom and they became very bold. . . . They were called followers of Wycliffe, Wychiffes or Lollards. . . . At the beginning the leaders of this dreadful sect used to wear russet clothes mostly, to show outwardly an inward simplicity of heart and thus exercise a subtle attraction, like wolves in sheep's clothing, in undyed wool. . . . They gained to their sect half or more than half the people, some genuinely, others intimidated or shamed into it, for they magnified their adherents as praiseworthy. . . . They always claimed to act under 'Goddislawe'.

Even the very recently converted strangely acquired a standard way of speaking in accordance with their tenets, and this change of language acted on Doctors and women alike. . . . It divided families and neighbour from neighbour. . . . They were very argumentative with plenty to say. . . .

There was at Leicester a priest call William de Swynderby whom the people called a hermit because he once lived as such. His antecedents are unknown, but it is remarkable how unstable were his life and manners, ever chopping and changing. . . . First he preached against female vanity and dress. Although they behaved well he did not know how to stop, and at last he made the women of the town, good and bad, so cross that they decided to stone him out of town.

Seeing his theme unprofitable he turned his sermons against the merchants saying a rich man could not enter the kingdom of God. He doled out this stuff so often that but for God's mercy he would have reduced some worthy man to the sin of desperation. Then he turned hermit, as preaching had not helped him. He lived for a while at a hermitage in the duke's wood, sometimes trotting into the town or the country. The pious of Leicester took the trouble to bring him food as usual, but he must needs refuse it saying that what little he had with the duke's help would suffice. He began to run short and to be bored, but shame kept him from moving back to town. He managed to get taken into the abbey there for a time, for the canons put him in a room in the church because they had hopes of his holiness and they supplied him like the other priests. At that time he visited the country churches. . . . He joined up with William Smith at St. John Baptist's by the leper hospital and associated there with other Wycliffes. At that time the sect was growing so much in repute and number that you could hardly see two people in the street but one was a Wycliffe. He saw that his usual kinds of sermons were unpopular and did not attract converts; so he levelled them against the clergy saying they were bad, and, as the rest of the sect, said parishioners need not pay tithes to the impure, to non-residents, or those prevented from teaching and preaching by ignorance or inaudibility, for the other Wycliffes said tithes were a voluntary gift and payment to evil-livers was connivance. He also preached that men might ask for payment of debt but not sue or imprison for it, that excommunication for non-payment of tithes was extortion and that one who lived contrary to God's law was no priest though ordained.

Such and other teachings and heresies pleased the people and won their affection. They said they had never seen or heard such an exponent of truth and they loved him like another God.

John Bukkyngham, Bishop of Lincoln, had wind of this and promptly suspended him from all preaching in chapel, church or graveyard, excommunicating any who should listen to him and sending notices of this to various churches. William set himself up a pulpit between two millstones which stood for sale outside the chapel in the High Street, to preach 'in the High Street in the bishop's teeth so long as he have the people's love'. You would have seen crowds from all over the town and country flocking to hear him more than even before the excommunication. The bishop summoned him to appear in Lincoln Cathedral. . . . There he was publicly convicted of heresies and errors and richly deserved to be food for fire. Then his followers cast their hands and heads in wailing to the walls, for many Leicester people would have gone to succour him, though in vain. That day the pious Duke of Lancaster happened to be at Lincoln and he often protected the Lollards, for their smooth tongues and faces tricked him and others into thinking them saints of God. He persuaded the bishop to give William a different sentence. . . .

ii. *Source: Register of the Bishop of Norwich*, quoted G. G. Coulton, *op. cit.*, pp. 462–5

'. . . the said Margery Backster did inform this deponent, that she should in no case swear; saying to her in English: 'Dame, beware of the bee, for every bee will sting; and therefore take heed you swear not, neither by God, neither by our lady, neither by any other saint; and if ye do contrary, the bee will sting your tongue and venom your soul.'

Item. This deponent being demanded by the said Margery, what she did every day at church; she answered, that she kneeled down and said five *Pater-Nosters*, in worship of the crucifix, and as many *Ave Marias* in worship of our lady. Whom Margery rebuked, saying, 'You do evil to kneel or pray to such images in the churches, for God swelleth not in such churches, neither shall he come down out of heaven; and he will give you no more reward for such prayer, than a candle lighted, and set under the cover of the font, will give light by night to those who are in the church': saying, moreover, in English: 'Lewdwrights[1] of stocks hew and form such crosses and images, and, after that, lewd painters gleer[2] them with colours. And if you desire so much to see the true cross of Christ, I will show it you at home in your own house.' Which this deponent being

1. ignorant carpenters.
2. gloss.

121

desirous to see, the said Margery, stretching out her arms abroad, said to this deponent: 'This is the true cross of Christ, and this cross thou oughtest and mayest every day behold and worship in thine own house; and therefore it is but vain to run to the church, to worship dead crosses and images.'

Item. This deponent, being demanded by the said Margery how she believed touching the sacrament of the altar, said that she believed the sacrament of the altar, after the consecration, to be the very body of Christ in form of bread. To whom Margery said: 'Your belief is nought. For if every sacrament were God, and the very body of Christ, there should be an infinite number of gods, because that a thousand priests, and more, do every day make a thousand such gods, and afterwards eat them, and void them out again in places where, if you will seek them, you may find many such gods. And, therefore, know for certainty, that by the grace of God it shall never be my god, because it is falsely and deceitfully ordained by the priests in the church, to induce the simple people to idolatry; for it is only material bread.'

Moreover, the said Margery said to this deponent, that Thomas of Canterbury, whom the people called Saint Thomas, was a false traitor, and damned in hell, because he injuriously endowed the churches with possessions, and raised up many heresies in the church, which seduce the simple people; and, therefore, if God be blessed, the said Thomas is accursed; and those false priests that say that he suffered his death patiently before the altar, do lie; for, as a false cowardly traitor, he was slain in the church door, as he was flying away.

Moreover, this deponent saith, that the said Margery told her, that the cursed pope, cardinals, archbishop, and bishops, and especially the bishop of Norwich, and others that support and maintain heresies and idolatry, reigning and ruling over the people, shall shortly have the very same or worse mischief fall upon them, than that cursed man, Thomas of Canterbury had. For they falsely and cursedly deceive the people with their false mammetries[1] and laws, to extort money from the simple folk, to sustain their pride, riot and idleness. And know assuredly that the vengeance of God will

1. idolatries.

speedily come upon them, who have most cruelly slain the children of God, Father Abraham, and William White, a true preacher of the law of God, and John Wadden, with many other godly men; which vengeance had come upon the said Caiaphas, the bishop of Norwich, and his ministers, who are members of the devil, before this time, if the pope had not sent over these false pardons unto those parties, which the said Caiaphas had falsely obtained, to induce the people to make procession for the state of them and of the church; which pardons brought the simple people to cursed idolatry.

Item, The said Margery said to this deponent, that every faithful man or woman is not bound to fast in Lent, or on other days appointed for fasting by the church; and that every man may lawfully eat flesh and all other meats upon the said days and times; and that it were better to eat the fragments left upon Thursday at night on the fasting days, than to go to the market to bring themselves in debt to buy fish; and that pope Silvester made the Lent.

Item, The said Margery said to this deponent, that William White was falsely condemned for a heretic, and that he was a good and holy man; and that he willed her to follow him to the place of execution, where she saw that when he would have opened his mouth to speak unto the people to instruct them, a devil (one of bishop Caiaphas's servants), struck him on the lips, and stopped his mouth, that he could in no case declare the will of God.

Item, this deponent saith, that the said Margery taught her, that she should not go on pilgrimage, neither to our lady of Walsingham, nor to any other saint or place.

Also this deponent saith, that the said Margery desired her, that she and Joan her maid would come secretly, in the night, to her chamber, and there she should hear her husband read the law of Christ unto them, which law was written in a book that her husband was wont to read to her by night: and that her husband is well learned in the christian verity. . . .

Item, She said moreover to this deponent, that holy bread and holy water were but trifles of no effect or force; and that the bells are to be cast out of the church, and that they are excommunicated who first ordained them.

Moreover, that she should not be burned, although she were

convicted of Lollardry, for that she had a charter of salvation in her body.

Also the said deponent saith, that Agnes Berthem, her servant, being sent to the house of the said Margery the Saturday after Ash-Wednesday, the said Margery not being within, found a brass pot standing over the fire, with a piece of bacon and oatmeal seething on it; as the said Agnes reported to this deponent.

✦

The Burning of Heretics (1401)

Source: Statutes of the Realm (1810–28), Vol. II p. 125, trans. C. Stephenson and F. G. Marcham, *op. cit.*, pp. 274–5

. . . With regard to which innovations and excesses [of the Lollards] set forth above, the prelates and clergy aforesaid, and also the commons of the said realm assembled in the same parliament, prayed the said lord king that his royal highness would in the said parliament deign to make provision for a suitable remedy. The same lord king then . . . by the assent of the magnates and other nobles of the said realm assembled in parliament, has granted, ordained, and established . . . that no one within the said kingdom or the other dominions subject to his royal majesty shall presume to preach in public or in secret without having first sought and obtained the licence of the local diocesan, always excepting curates in their own churches, persons who have hitherto enjoyed the privilege, and others to whom it has been granted by canon law; and that henceforth no one either openly or secretly shall preach, hold, teach, or impart anything, or compose or write any book, contrary to the catholic faith or the decisions of Holy Church, or anywhere hold conventicles or in any way have or maintain schools for such a sect and its nefarious doctrines and opinions; and also that in the future no one shall favour anybody who thus preaches, holds such or similar conventicles, has or maintains such schools, composes or writes such a book, or in any such fashion teaches, instructs, or excites the people. . . . And if any person within the said kingdom and dominions is formally convicted before the local diocesan or commissioners of the said nefarious preachings, doctrines, opinions, [holding of] schools, and heretical and erroneous instruction, or any of them, and if he refuses properly to abjure the same . . . or, after abjuration has been made by the same person, he is declared by the local diocesan or his commissioners to have relapsed, so that according to the sacred canons he ought to be relinquished to the secular court . . ., then the sheriff of the local county and the mayor and sheriffs or sheriff, or the mayor and bailiffs of the city, town, or borough of the same county nearest the said diocesan or his said commissioners . . . shall, after the pronouncement of such sentences, receive those persons and every one of them and shall have them burned before the people in some prominent place, so that such punishment shall inspire fear in the minds of others and prevent such nefarious doctrines and heretical and erroneous opinions, or their authors and protagonists in the said kingdom and dominions, from being supported or in any way tolerated against the catholic faith, the Christian religion, and the decisions of Holy Church— which God forbid! And in all and singular of the aforesaid matters regarding the said ordinance and statute, the sheriffs, mayors, and bailiffs of the counties, cities, towns, and boroughs aforesaid are to be attentive, helpful, and favourable to the said diocesans and their commissioners.

◆

The Execution of Sir John Oldcastle
(1413)

*Source: London Chronicle Julius B.*11, quoted J. J. Bagley, *Historical Interpretation* (1965), p. 220

In this same year, thanked be Almighty God, the general council was ended and union made in holy church: and a pope chosen at Constance upon St. Martin's Day by the assent of all the general council, and he is called Martin V. Also in the same year was Sir John Oldcastle, called the Lord Cobham, taken in the Marches of Wales and brought to the City of London, the which was chief lord maintainer of all the Lollards in this realm, and ever about to destroy to his power holy church. And therefore he was first drawn, and afterwards hanged, and burnt hanging on the new gallows besides St. Giles with an iron chain about his neck, because that he was a lord of name. And so there he made an end of his cursed life.

❖

Censorship for Heresy at Cambridge
(1384)

Source: 'Speculum Vitae', MS Bodley 446 folio 1, quoted and trans. W. A. Pantin, *The English Church in the Fourteenth Century* (1962), p. 229

In the year of Our Lord 1384, this compilation was examined at Cambridge in this manner. While it was left there by a certain priest, in order to be bound, it was carefully looked at by certain scholars, and read through and presented to the Chancellor of the University and his Council, in order to be examined for defects and heresies, lest the unlearned should carelessly deceive the people through its means, and fallaciously lead them into various errors. Then by command of the Chancellor, before him and the whole Council of the University, it was examined for four days with all care and diligence, and tested in every college on every side, and on the fifth day all the doctors of both laws and the masters of theology, together with the Chancellor, declared and affirmed that it was well and subtly drawn out of the sacred laws and divine books, and that it was alleged, affirmed and founded on the authority of all the Doctors of the Sacred Page. Therefore whoever you are, O reader, do not despise this work, because without a doubt, if any defects had been found in it, it would have been burnt before the University of Cambridge.

❖

Pilgrimage in the Fourteenth Century

Source: Geoffrey Chaucer, *Canterbury Tales,* ed. N. Coghill (1951), pp. 25–6

> Then people long to go on pilgrimages
> And palmers long to seek the stranger strands
> Of far-off saints, hallowed in sundry lands,
> And specially, from every shire's end
> In England, down to Canterbury they wend
> To seek the holy blissful martyr, quick
> In giving help to them when they were sick.
>   It happened in that season that one day
> In Southwark, at The Tabard, as I lay
> Ready to go on pilgrimage and start
> For Canterbury, most devout at heart,
> At night there came into that hostelry

Some nine and twenty in a company
Of sundry folk happening then to fall
In fellowship, and they were pilgrims all
That towards Canterbury meant to ride.

❖

Becket's Shrine

Source: Relation of England, trans. G. G. Coulton, *Social Life in Britain from the Conquest to the Reformation* (1918), pp. 39–40

I saw, one day (being with your Magnificence at Westminster, a place out of London) the tomb of the Saint King Edward the Confessor, in the church of the aforesaid place Westminster; and indeed, neither St. Martin of Tours, a church in France, which I have heard is one of the richest in existence, nor anything else that I have ever seen, can be put into any sort of comparison with it. But the magnificence of the tomb of St. Thomas the Martyr, Archbishop of Canterbury, is that which surpasses all belief. This, notwithstanding its great size, is entirely covered over with plates of pure gold; but the gold is scarcely visible from the variety of precious stones with which it is studded, such as sapphires, diamonds, rubies, balas-rubies,[1] and emeralds; and on every side that the eye turns, something more beautiful than the other appears. And these beauties of nature are enhanced by human skill, for the gold is carved and engraved in beautiful designs, both large and small, and agates, jaspers and cornelians set *in relievo*, some of the cameos being of such a size, that I do not dare to mention it: but everything is left far behind by a ruby, not larger than a man's thumb-nail, which is set to the right of the altar. The church is rather dark, and particu-

1 A delicate rose-red variety of ruby.

larly so where the shrine is placed, and when we went to see it the sun was nearly gone down, and the weather was cloudy; yet I saw that ruby as well as if I had it in my hand; they say that it was the gift of a king of France.

◆

Three Canterbury Pilgrims

I. A MONK

Source: Geoffrey Chaucer, *Canterbury Tales*, ed. N. Coghill (1951), pp. 29–30

There was a Monk, a leader of the fashions;
Inspecting farms and hunting were his passions,
Fit to be Abbot, a manly man and able.
Many the dainty horses in his stable;
His bridle, when he rode, a man might hear
Jingling in a whistling wind as clear,
Aye, and as loud as does the chapel bell
Where my lord Monk was Prior of the cell.
The Rule of good St. Benet or St. Maur
As old and strict he tended to ignore;
He let go by the things of yesterday
And followed the new world's more spacious way.
He did not rate that text at a plucked hen
Which says that hunters are not holy men.

· · · · · · · · · · · · · ·

This Monk was therefore a good man to horse;
Greyhounds he had, as swift as birds, to course.
Hunting a hare or riding at a fence
Was all his fun, he spared for no expense.

I saw his sleeves were garnished at the hand
With fine grey fur, the finest in the land,
And where his hood was fastened at his chin
He had a wrought-gold cunningly fashioned pin.
Into a lover's knot it seemed to pass.
His head was bald and shone as any glass,
So did his face, as if it had been greased.
He was a fat and personable priest;
His bright eyes rolled, they never seemed to settle,
And glittered like the flames beneath a kettle;
Supple his boots, his horse in fine condition.
He was a prelate fit for exhibition,
He was not pale like a tormented soul.
He liked a fat swan best, and roasted whole.

2. A PRIORESS

Source: Geoffrey Chaucer, *op. cit.,* pp. 28–9

There also was a Nun, a Prioress;
Simple her way of smiling was and coy.
Her greatest oath was only 'By St. Loy!'
And she was known as Madam Eglantyne.
And well she sang a service, with a fine
Intoning through her nose, as was most seemly,
And she spoke daintily in French, extremely,
After the school at Stratford-atte-Bowe;
French in the Paris style she did not know.
At meat her manners were well taught withal;
No morsel from her lips did she let fall,
Nor dipped her fingers in the sauce too deep;
But she could carry a morsel up and keep
The smallest drop from falling on her breast.
For courtliness she had a special zest.
And she would wipe her upper lip so clean
That not a trace of grease was to be seen

Upon the cup when she had drunk; to eat,
She reached a hand sedately for the meat.
She certainly was very entertaining,
Pleasant and friendly in her ways, and straining
To counterfeit a courtly kind of grace,
A stately bearing fitting to her place,
And to seem dignified in all her dealings.
As for her sympathies and tender feelings,
She was so charitably solicitous
She used to weep if she but saw a mouse
Caught in a trap, if it were dead or bleeding.
And she had little dogs she would be feeding
With roasted flesh, or milk, or fine white bread.
Sorely she wept if one of them were dead
Or someone took a stick and made it smart;
She was all sentiment and tender heart.
Her veil was gathered in a seemly way,
Her nose was elegant, her eyes glass-grey;
Her mouth was very small, but soft and red,
And certainly she had a well-shaped head,
Almost a span across the brows, I own;
She was indeed by no means undergrown.
Her cloak I noticed, had a graceful charm.
She wore a coral trinket on her arm,
A set of beads, the gaudies tricked in green,
Whence hung a golden brooch of brightest sheen
On which there first was graven a crowned A,
And lower, *Amor vincit omnia.*

3. A PARDONER

Source: op. cit., p. 44

There was no pardoner of equal grace,
For in his trunk he had a pillow-case
Which he asserted was Our Lady's veil.

He said he had a gobbet of the sail
Saint Peter had the time when he made bold
To walk the waves, till Jesu Christ took hold.
He had a cross of metal set with stones
And, in a glass, a rubble of pigs' bones.
And with these relics, any time he found
Some poor up-country parson to astound,
On one short day, in money down, he drew
More than the parson in a month or two,
And by his flatteries and prevarication
Made monkeys of the priest and congregation.
But still to do him justice first and last
In church he was a noble ecclesiast.
How well he read a lesson or told a story!
But best of all he sang an Offertory,
For well he knew that when that song was sung
He'd have to preach and tune his honey-tongue
And well he could win silver from the crowd.
That's why he sang so merrily and loud.

❖

Piety and Images

Source: Historie of the Arrivall of Edward IV, ed. J. Bruce (1838), p. 15, quoted J. R. Lander, *The Wars of the Roses* (1965), pp. 182–3

So it fell, that, the same Palm Sunday, the king [Edward IV] went in procession, and all the people after, in good devotion, as the service of that day asketh, and, when the procession was comen into the church, and, by order of the service, were comen to that place where the veil should be drawn up afore the Rood, that all the people shall honour the Rood, with the anthem, *Ave*, three times began, in a pillar of the church, directly aforn the place where the king kneeled, and devoutly honoured the Rood, was a little image of Saint Anne, made of alabaster, standing fixed to the pillar, closed and clasped together, with four boards, small, painted, and going round about the image, in manner of a compass, like as it is to see commonly, and all about, where as such images be wont to be made for to be sold and set up in churches, capels, crosses, and oratories, in many places. And this image was thus shut, closed, and clasped, according to the rules that, in all the churches of England, be observed, all images to be hid from Ash Wednesday to Easter Day in the morning. And so the said image had been from Ash Wednesday to that time. And even suddenly, at that season of the service, the boards compassing the image about gave a great crack, and a little opened, which the king well-perceived and all the people about him. And anon, after, the boards drew and closed together again, without any man's hand, or touching, and, as though it had been a thing done with a violence, with a greater might it opened all abroad, and so the image stood, open and discovered, in sight of all the people there being. The king, this seeing, thanked and honoured God, and Saint Anne, taking it for a good sign, and token of good and prosperous adventure that God would send him in that he had to do. . . .

❖

Chantries

1. ARCHBISHOP ZOUCHE OF YORK (1342–52)

Source: Register, folio 49, E. F. Jacob, *The Fifteenth Century* (1961), p. 291

It is befitting to encourage with affectionate sympathy the sincere devotion of those who desire to give of their worldly goods to the increase of divine worship, the multiplication of the number of them who minister in God's holy church, and the establishment of celebrations of masses which are the more profitable to Christ's faithful unto salvation, inasmuch as in the same the King of Heaven is placated by mystic gifts, and remedies for sin are more easily obtained by asking.

2. A FOURTEENTH CENTURY MAYOR OF YORK

Source: York Memorandum Book, ed. M. Sellers (1911–15) Vol. II p. 19, quoted K. L. Wood-Legh, *Perpetual Chantries* (1965), p. 181

The priests of this city and suburbs having chantries, and others, stipendiaries, who have not such chantries, are the special orators of the citizens their patrons and masters, from whom they have, and have had, their chantries and stipends from which they live.

❖

Two Devout Fifteenth Century Laywomen

1. CICELY, DUCHESS OF YORK

Source: A collection of Ordinances and Regulations for the Government of the Royal Household (1790), p. 37, quoted W. A. Pantin, *The English Church in the Fourteenth Century* (1962), p. 154

Me seemeth it is requisite to understand the order of her own person concerning God and the world. She useth to arise at seven of the clock, and hath ready her chaplain to say with her matins of the day and matins of Our Lady; and when she is full ready, she hath a low Mass in her chamber, and after Mass she taketh somewhat to recreate nature; and so goeth to the chapel, hearing the divine service and two low Masses, from thence to dinner, during the time whereof she hath a reading of holy matter, either Hilton *Of Active and Contemplative Life*, Bonaventure *De infancia Salvatoris*, the *Golden Legend*, St. Maud [Mechtild], St. Katherine of Siena, or the *Revelations* of St. Brigit.

After dinner she giveth audience to all such as have any matter to show unto her, by the space of one hour; and then she sleepeth one quarter of an hour; and after she hath slept, she continueth in prayer unto the first peal of evensong; then she drinketh wine or ale at her pleasure. Forthwith her chaplain is ready to say with her both evensongs; and after the last peal she goeth to the chapel and heareth evensong by note [sung]; from thence to supper, and in the time of supper, she reciteth the reading that was had at dinner to those that be in her presence.

After supper she disposeth herself to be familiar with her gentle women, to the following of honest mirth; and one hour before her going to bed, she taketh a cup of wine, and after that goeth to her private closet and taketh her leave of God for all night, making an end of her prayers for that day, and by eight of the clock is in bed. I trust to Our Lord's mercy that this noble princess thus divideth the hours to His High pleasure.

2. MARGERY KEMPE

Source: The Book of Margery Kempe, ed. W. Butler-Bowdon (1954), pp. 215, 99.

When she was there [in the Priory cloister at St. Margaret's, Lynn], she had so great mind of the Passion of Our Lord Jesu Christ and of His precious wounds and how dearly He bought her, that she cried and roared wonderfully, so that she might be heard a great way off, and might not restrain herself therefrom. Then had she great wonder how Our Lady might suffer or endure to see His precious body be scourged and hanged on the cross. Also it came to her mind how men had said to her before, that Our Lady, Christ's own Mother, cried not as she did, and that caused her to say in her crying, 'Lord, I am not Thy Mother. Take away this pain from me, for I may not bear it. Thy passion will slay me.' Then there came by her a wonderful clerk, a doctor of divinity, and said, 'I had sooner than twenty pounds that I might have such a sorrow for Our Lord's Passion.'

And the woman that had the image in the chest, when they came into good cities, she took the image out of her chest, and set it in the laps of worshipful wives; and they would put clothes upon it, and kiss it as though it had been God Himself. And when the creature [i.e. Margery] saw the worship and the reverence that they did to the image, she was taken with such sweet devotion and sweet meditations that she wept with great sobbing and loud crying. And she was moved so much the more, because while she was in England, she had high meditations on the birth and childhood of Christ, and she thanked God forasmuch as she saw these creatures have so great faith in what she saw with her bodily eye, like as she had before with her ghostly eye.

❖

Benefit of Clergy

Source: Relation of England, trans. G. G. Coulton, *Social Life in Britain from the Conquest to the Reformation* (1918), pp. 41–2

In another way, also, the priests are the occasion of crimes; in that they have usurped a privilege that no thief or murderer who can read, should perish by the hands of justice; and, when anyone is condemned to death by the sentence of the twelve men of the robe, if the criminal can read, he asks to defend himself by the book; when, a psalter, or missal, or some other ecclesiastical book, being brought to him, if he can read it he is liberated from the power of the law, and given as a clerk into the hands of the bishop. But, not-withstanding all these evasions, people are taken up every day by dozens, like birds in a covey, and especially in London; yet, for all this, they never cease to rob and murder in the streets. And if the King should propose to change any old established rule, it would seem to every Englishman as if his life were taken from him; but I think that the present King Henry [VII] will do away with a great many, should he live ten years longer.

3

LAND AND PEOPLE

❖

Fifteenth Century Views of England

i. *Source: Relation of England*, quoted J. R. Lander, *The Wars of the Roses* (1965), pp. 310–11

The riches of England are greater than those of any other country in Europe, as I have been told by the oldest and most experienced merchants, and also as I myself can vouch, from what I have seen. This is owing in the first place, to the great fertility of the soil, which is such, that, with the exception of wine, they import nothing from abroad for their subsistence. Next, the sale of their valuable tin brings in a large sum of money to the kingdom; but still more do they derive from their extraordinary abundance of wool, which bears such a high price and reputation throughout Europe. And in order to keep the gold and silver in the country, when once it has entered, they have made a law, which has been in operation for a long time now, that no money, nor gold nor silver plate should be carried out of England under a very heavy penalty. And every one who makes a tour in the island will soon become aware of this great wealth, as will have been the case with your Magnificence, for there is no small innkeeper, however poor and humble he may be, who does not serve his table with silver dishes and drinking cups; and no one, who has not in his house silver plate to the amount of at least £100 sterling, which is equivalent to 500 golden crowns with us, is considered by the English to be a person of any consequence. But above all are their riches displayed in the church treasures; for there is not a parish church in the kingdom so mean as not to possess crucifixes, candlesticks, censers, patens and cups of silver; nor is there a convent of mendicant friars so poor, as not to have all these same articles in silver, besides many other ornaments worthy of a cathedral church in the same metal. Your Magnificence may therefore imagine what the decorations of those enormously rich Benedictine, Carthusian and Cistercian monasteries must be. These are, indeed, more like baronial palaces than religious houses. . . .

ii. *Source:* Sir John Fortescue, *De Legibus Legum Anglie,* quoted J. R. Lander, *op. cit.,* pp. 302–8

. . . You remember, most admirable prince, you have seen how rich in fruits are the villages and towns of the kingdom of France, whilst you were travelling there, but so burdened by the men-at-arms, and their horses, of the king of that land, that you could be entertained in scarcely any of them except the great towns. There you learned from the inhabitants that those men, though they might be quartered in one village for a month or two, paid or wished to pay absolutely nothing for the expense of themselves and their horses, and, what is worse, they compelled the inhabitants of the villages and towns on which they descended to supply them at their own charges with wines, meats and other things which they required. . . .

. . . In the realm of England, no one billets himself in another's house against its master's will, unless in public hostelries, where even so he will pay in full for all that he has expended there, before his departure thence; nor does anyone take with impunity the goods of another without the permission of the proprietor of them; nor, in that realm, is anyone hindered from providing himself with salt or any goods whatever, at his own pleasure and of any vendor. The king, indeed, may, by his officers, take necessaries for his household, at a reasonable price to be assessed at the discretion of the constables of the villages, without the owner's permission. But nonetheless he is obliged by his own laws to pay this price out of hand or at a day fixed by the greater officers of his household, because by those laws he cannot despoil any of his subjects of their goods without due satisfaction for them. Nor does the king there, by himself or by his ministers, impose tallages, subsidies, or any other burdens whatever on his subjects, nor change their laws, nor make new ones, without the concession or assent of his whole realm expressed in parliament. . . .

. . . Hence the inhabitants of that land are rich, abounding in gold and silver and all the necessaries of life. They do not drink water, except those who sometimes abstain from other drinks by way of devotional or penitential zeal. They eat every kind of flesh and fish in abundance, with which their land is not meanly stocked. They are clothed with good woollens throughout their garments; they have abundant bedding, woollen like the rest of their furnishings, in all their houses, and are rich in all household goods and agricultural equipment, and in all that is requisite for a quiet and happy life, according to their estate.

iii. *Source: Relation of England*, quoted J. R. Lander, *op. cit.*, pp. 300–1

It is the easiest thing in the world to get a person thrown into prison in this country; for every officer of justice, both civil and criminal, has the power of arresting anyone, at the request of a private individual, and the accused person cannot be liberated without giving security, unless he be acquitted by the judgement of a jury of twelve men; nor is there any punishment awarded for making a slanderous accusation. Such severe measures against criminals ought to keep the English in check, but, for all this, there is no country in the world where there are so many thieves and robbers as in England; insomuch, that few venture to go alone in the country, excepting in the middle of the day, and fewer still in the towns at night, and least of all in London.

. . . people are taken up every day by dozens, like birds in a covey, and especially in London; yet, for all this, they never cease to rob and murder in the streets.

The West Country

Sources: i. letter of Adam Marsh, c. 1240, trans. G. G. Coulton, *op. cit.,* p. 26

ii. letter of John Grandisson, Bishop of Exeter (1327–69), trans. G. G. Coulton, *op. cit.,* p. 27

i. I have not yet fully conferred with Master Robert Marsh (my brother) concerning persons apt for the prebend for which you have asked me to recommend. But, as I now see the matter, there occurs to me Master Solomon of Dover . . . Master Peter of Aldham . . . and Master Richard of Cornwall, who, reverend Father, is not altogether unknown to you; a man lacking in command of the English tongue, yet of most honest conversation and unblemished reputation, learned in human and divine literature.

ii. Purposing to survey the possessions and buildings appertaining to my see, I travelled to the border parts of Cornwall. That land adjoineth England only with its eastern boundary; the rest is everywhere surrounded by the ocean, far beyond which, to the North, lie Wales and Ireland. Southwards, it looks straight over to Gascony and Brittany; and the men of Cornwall speak the Breton tongue. To the West of St. Michael's Mount, the immensity of ocean stretches without bound or limit. My see possesseth also certain sea-girt islands [i.e. Scilly], whereunto no bishop ever goeth, but they have been wont to send a few friars, as I have not [yet] done.

Here I am not only at the end of the world but even (if I may say so) at the ends of the very end. For this diocese, which includes Devon and Cornwall, is divided from the rest of England, and girt on all sides but one by an ocean which is rarely navigable, and frequented only by the natives of the land. It aboundeth sufficiently in home fed flesh of beasts and at times in Gascony wine; but it is less fertile in corn and other things necessary to man. My episcopal manors I found terribly destroyed and despoiled, in hatred of my predecessor who was so inhumanly murdered, my lands waste and untilled, and an utter default of cattle and seed corn.

The Use of French in Courts Discontinued (1362)

Source: Statutes of the Realm (1810–28), Vol. I pp. 375–6, trans. C. Stephenson and F. G. Marcham, *op. cit.*, p. 231

Item, because it is often showed to the king by the prelates, dukes, earls, barons, and all the commonalty, of the great mischiefs which have happened to divers of the realm, because the laws, customs and statutes of this realm be not commonly known in the same realm, for that they be pleaded, showed and judged in the French tongue, which is much unknown in the said realm; so that the people which do implead, or be impleaded, in the king's court, and in the courts of other have no knowledge nor understanding of that which is said for them or against them by their sergeants and other pleaders; and that reasonably the said laws and customs shall be the more soon learned and known, and better understood in the tongue used in the said realm, and by so much every man of the said realm may the better govern himself without offending of the law, and the better keep, save, and defend his heritage and possessions; and in divers regions and countries where the king, the nobles, and other of the said realm have been, good governance and full right is done to every person, because that their laws and customs be learned and used in the tongue of the country, the king desiring the good governance and tranquillity of his people, and to put out and eschew the harms and mischiefs which do or may happen in this behalf by the occasions aforesaid, hath ordained and established by the assent aforesaid, that all pleas which shall be pleaded in his court whatsoever, before any of his justices whatsoever, or in his other places, or before any of his other ministers whatsoever, or in the courts and places of any other lords whatsoever within the realm, shall be pleaded, showed, defended, answered, debated, and judged in the English tongue, and that they be entered and inrolled in Latin, and that the laws and customs of the same realm, terms, and processes, be holden and kept as they be and have been before this time; and that by the ancient terms and form of pleaders no man be prejudiced, so that the matter of the action be fully showed in the declaration and in the writ: and it accorded by the assent aforesaid, that this ordinance and statute of pleading begin and hold place at the fifteenth of Saint Hilary next coming.

✦

Language in Fourteenth Century England

Source: John of Trevisa, *Descrypcion of Englonde*, quoted G. G. Coulton, *Social Life in Britain from the Conquest to the Reformation* (1918), pp. 5–7

How meny manere peple beeth in this ilond, there beeth also so many dyvers langages and tonges; notheles Walsche men and Scottes, that beeth nought i-medled with other naciouns, holdeth wel nyh thir firste longage and speche; but yet the Scottes, that were somtyme confederat and wonede with the Pictes, drawe somwhat after thir speche; but the Flemmynges that live in the weste side of Wales haveth i-left ther straunge speche and speketh Saxonliche i-now. Also Englische men, (though thei hadde from the bygynnynge thre manere speche, northerne, sowtherne, and middel speche in the myddel of the lond, as they come of thre manere peple of Germania,) notheles by comyxtioun and mellynge firste with Danes and afterward with Normans, in many thynges the contray longage is impayred, and som useth straunge whafferynge, chiterynge, harrynge, and garrynge grisbayting.[1] This impayrynge of the truthe of the tongue is bycause of tweie thinges, oon is for children

1. gabbling, chattering, snarling, croaking, and hissing.

143

in scole, agenst the usage and manere of alle othere naciouns, beeth compelled for to leve thire owne langage, and for to construe thir lessouns and there thynges in Frensche, and so they haveth seth the Normans come first in to Engelond. Also gentil men children beeth i-taught to speke Frensche from the tyme that they beeth i-rokked in their cradel and kunneth speke and playe with a childes broche; and uplondisshe men wil likne thym self to gentil men, and fondeth[1] with greet besynesse for to speke Frensce for to be i-tolde of. This manere was moche i-used to fore the firste moreyn[2] and is sithe sumdel i-chaunged; for John Cornwaile, a maister of grammar, chaunged the lore in gramer scole and construccioun of Frensche into Englische; and Richard Pencriche lerned that manere techynge of hym and othere men of Pencrich; so that now, the yere of oure Lorde a thowsand thre hundred and foure score and fyve, and of the secounde kyng Richard after the conquest nyne, in alle the gramere scoles of Engelond, children leveth Frensche and con-strueth and lerneth an Englische, and haveth therby avauntage in oon side and disavauntage in another side; here avauntage is, that they lerneth ther gramer in lasse tyme than children were i-woned to doo; disavauntage is that now children of gramer scole conneth na more Frensche than can thir lift heele; and that is harme for them and they schulle passe the see and travaille in straunge landes and in many other places. Also gentil men haveth now moche i-left for to teche there children Frensche. Hit semeth a greet wonder how Englische, that is the burthe tonge of Englisshemen and her owne langage and tonge, is so dyverse of sown in this oon ilond, and the langage of Normandie is comlynge of[3] another londe, and hath oon manere soun among alle men that speketh hit aright in Engelond. Nevertheles there is as many dyvers maner Frensche in the reem of Fraunce as duvers manere Englische in the reem of Engelond. Also of the forsaide Saxon tonge that is i-deled a-thre, and is abide scarsliche with fewe uplondisshe men, is greet wonder; for men of the est with men of the west, as it were undir the same partie of hevene, accordeth more in sownynge of speche than men of the

1. strive.
2. plague.
3. imported from.

north with men of the south; therfore it is that Mercii, that beeth men of myddel Engelond, as it were parteners of the endes, understondeth bettre the side langages, northerne and southerne, than northerne or southerne understondeth either other. Al the longage of the Northumbres, and specialliche at York, is so scharp, slitting, and frotynge[1] and vnschape, that we southerne men may that longage unnethe understonde. I trowe that that is bycause that they beeth nyh to straunge men and naciouns that speketh strongliche, and also bycause that the kunges of Engelond woneth alwey fer from that cuntrey; for they beeth more i-torned to the south contray, and yif they gooth to the north contray they gooth with greet help and strengthe.

❖

Meals and Manners

Source: John of Trevisa, *Bartholomew the Englishman,* Vol. VI ch. 23-4, quoted G. G. Coulton, *op. cit.,* pp. 373-5

. . . at feasts first meat is prepared and arranged, then guests are called together, forms and stools set in the hall, and tables, cloths and towels ordained, dispersed and made ready. Guests are sat with the lord in the chief place of the board, and they sit not down at the board before the guests wash their hands. Children are sat in their place, and servants at a table by themselves. First knives, spoons and salts are set on the board, and then bread and drink and many different dishes. Household servants busily help each other to everything diligently, and talk merrily together. The guests are gladdened with lutes and harps. Now wine and dishes of meat are brought forth and despatched. At the last cometh fruit and spices, and then they have eaten, board cloths and scraps are borne away, and guests wash and wipe their hands again. Then graces are said and guests thank the Lord. Then for gladness and comfort drink is

1. grating.

brought yet again. At the end men take their leave, and some go to bed and sleep, and some go home to their own lodgings.

All that is rehearsed before of dinners and feasts accordeth to the supper also. Many things are necessary and proper for supper. . . .

The first is convenient time, . . . not too early, not too late. The second is convenient place, large, pleasant and secure. . . . The third is the hearty and glad cheer of him that maketh the feast: the supper is not worthy to be praised if the lord of the house be heavy cheered. . . . The fourth is many divers dishes, so that who that will not of one may taste of another. . . . The fifth is divers wines and drinks. . . . The sixth is courtesy and honesty of servants. . . . The seventh is kind friendship and company of them that sit at the supper. . . . The eighth is mirth of song and of instruments of music: noble men use not to make suppers without harp or symphony. . . . The ninth is plenty of light of candles and tapers and of torches, for it is shame to sup in darkness and perilous also for flies and other filth. Therefore candles and tapers are set on candlesticks to burn. The tenth is the deliciousness of all that is set on the board, for it is not used at supper to serve men with great meat and common as it is used at dinner, but with special light meat and delicious. . . . The eleventh is long during of the supper, for men use after full end of work and travail to sit long at the supper. For meat eaten too hastily grieveth against night, therefore at the supper men should eat by leisure and not too hastily. . . . The twelfth is sureness, for without harm and damage every man shall be prayed to the supper, and after supper that is freely offered it is not honest to compel a man to pay his share. The thirteenth is softness and liking of rest and of sleep. After supper men shall rest, for then sleep is sweet and liking . . . for . . . when smoke of meat cometh into the brain, then men sleep easily.

A Fifteenth Century Menu for Stewed Partridge

Source: Historical Interpretation, J. J. Bagley (1965), p. 182

Take a moderately strong broth of beef or of mutton when it is boiled enough, and strain it through a strainer, and put it in an earthenware pot. And take a good quantity of wine, as it were half a pint. And take partridge, cloves, maces and whole pepper, and cast into the pot, and let boil well together. And when the partridge been enough, take the pot from the fire, and then take fair bread cut in thin browes and couch them in a fair charger, and lay the partridge on top. And take powder of ginger, salt, and hard yolks of eggs minced, and cast into the broth, and pour the broth upon the partridge into the charger, and serve it forth, but let it be coloured with saffron.

❖

English Towns in the Fifteenth Century

Source: Relation of England (1847), pp. 41–2, trans. G. G. Coulton, *op. cit.,* pp. 334–5

There are scarcely any towns of importance in the kingdom, excepting these two: Bristol, a seaport to the west, and Boraco [Eboracum] otherwise York which is on the borders of Scotland; besides London to the south. Eboracum was in ancient times the principal city of the island, and was adorned with many buildings by the Romans, in their elegant style, but having been sacked and burnt in the reign of King William the Conqueror, she never afterwards could recover her former splendour; so that, at present, all the beauty of this island is confined to London; which, although sixty miles distant from the sea, possesses all the advantages to be desired in a maritime town; being situated on the river Thames, which is very much affected by the tide, for many miles (I do not know the exact number) above it: and London is so much benefited by this ebb and flow of the river, that vessels of 100 tons burden can come up to the city, and ships of any size to within five miles of it; yet the water in this river is fresh for twenty miles below London. Although this city has no buildings in the Italian style, but of timber or brick like the French, the Londoners live comfortably, and, it appears to me, that there are not fewer inhabitants than at Florence or Rome. It abounds with every article of luxury, as well as with the necessaries of life: but the most remarkable thing in London is the wonderful quantity of wrought silver. I do not allude to that in private houses, (though the landlord of the house in which the Milanese ambassador lived, had plate to the amount of 100 crowns), but to the shops of London. In one single street, named the Strand, leading to St. Paul's, there are fifty-two gold-smith's shops, so rich and full of silver vessels, great and small, that in all the shops in Milan, Rome, Venice and Florence put together, I do not think there would be found so many of the magnificence that are to be seen in London. And these vessels are all either salt cellars, or drinking cups, or basins to hold water for the hands; for they eat off that fine tin [pewter] which is little inferior to silver. These great riches of London are not occasioned by its inhabitants being noblemen or gentlemen; being all, on the contrary, persons of low degree, and artificers who have congregated there from all parts of the island, and from Flanders, and from every other place. No one can be mayor or alderman of London, who has not been an apprentice in his youth; that is, who has not passed the seven or nine years in that hard service described before. Still, the citizens of London are thought quite as highly of there, as the Venetian gentlemen are at Venice, as I think your Magnificence may have perceived. The city is divided into several wards, each of which has six officers; but superior to these are twenty-four gentlemen who they call aldermen, which in their language signifies old or experienced men; and, of these aldermen, one is elected every year by themselves, to be a magistrate named the mayor, who is in no less

148

estimation with the Londoners, than the person of our most serene lord [the Doge] is with us, or than the Gonfaloniero at Florence; and the day on which he enters upon his office, he is obliged to give a sumptuous entertainment to all the principal people in London, as well as to foreigners of distinction; and I, being one of the guests, together with your Magnificence, carefully observed every room and hall, and the court, where the company were all seated, and was of opinion that there must have been 1000 or more persons at table. The dinner lasted four hours or more; but it is true that the dishes were not served with that assiduity and frequency that is the custom with us in Italy; there being long pauses between each course, the company conversing the while. A no less magnificent banquet is given when two other officers named sheriffs are appointed; to which I went, being anxious to see every thing well; your Magnificence also was invited but did not go in consequence of the invitation having come from the Lord Privy Seal. At this feast, I observed the infinite profusion of victuals, and of plate, which was for the most part gilt; and amongst other things, I noticed how punctiliously they sat in their order, and the extraordinary silence of every one, insomuch that I could have imagined it one of those public repasts of the Lacedemonians that I have read of.

❖

Municipal Ordinances at Leicester (1466–7)

Source: M. Bateson, *Records of the Borough of Leicester* (1899–1905), Vol. II pp. 285–6

The ordinance made by Richard Gillot, mayor of the town of Leicester, and his brethren, and by the advice and assent of all the commons of the same town, at a common hall held at Leicester the Thursday next before the feast of St. Simon and St. Jude, in the seventh year of the reign of our sovereign lord King Edward the Fourth after the Conquest of England.

The mayor commands, on the king's behalf, that all manner of men keep the peace of our sovereign lord the king, and that no man disturb it within the franchise of this town as by armour or weapon bearing . . . and that no man walk after nine of the bell be stricken in the night without light, or without reasonable cause, on pain of imprisonment. . . .

that all brewers that brew shall brew good ale, and see that it be neither raw, roppy, nor red, but wholesome for man's body, selling a gallon of the best for a penny halfpenny, a gallon of the second for a penny, and a gallon of the third for a halfpenny, and that they sell none by unlawful or unsealed measure, on pain of imprisonment. . . .

that no man or woman suffer any corruption to lie before his door, nor cast any out of his door by night or day—that is to say horse, swine, dog, cat, or any other corruption—within the four gates or within the four streets of the suburbs . . . [nor] sweep nor throw out sweepings when it rains upon his neighbour . . . on pain of imprisonment.

that no man of the town or the country play within the franchise of this town for silver at unlawful games—that is to say at dice, hasarding, tennis, bowls, picking with arrows, quoiting with horse-shoes, pennyprick, football, or checker in the mire, on pain of imprisonment. . . .

that no woman wash clothes or any other corruption at the common wells of the town, or in the high street, on pain of imprisonment.

❖

Town Sanitation (1388)

Source: Statutes of the Realm (1810–28), Vol. II p. 62, trans. G. G. Coulton, *op. cit.,* pp. 330–1

For that so much Dung and Filth of the Garbage and Intrails as well of Beasts killed, as of other Corruptions, be cast and put in Ditches, Rivers and other Waters, and also within many other Places, within, about and nigh unto divers Cities, Boroughs, and Towns of the Realm, and the suburbs of them, that the air there is greatly corrupt and infect, and many Maladies and other intolerable Diseases do daily happen, as well to the Inhabitants, and those that are conversant in the said Cities, Boroughs, Towns and Suburbs, as to others repairing and travelling thither, to the great Annoyance, Damage and Peril of the Inhabitants, Dwellers, Repairers and Travellers aforesaid: It is accorded and assented, That Proclamation be made as well in the City of London, as in other Cities, Boroughs, and Towns through the Realm of England, where it shall be needful, as well within Franchises as without, that all they which do cast and lay all such Annoyances, Dung, Garbages, Intrails, and other Ordure in Ditches, Rivers, Waters, and other Places aforesaid, shall cause them utterly to be removed, avoided, and carried away betwixt this and the Feast of St. Michael next ensuing after the end of this present Parliament, every one upon Pain to lose and forfeit to our Lord the King £20.

Cook-shops in 1378

Source: Memorials of London and London Life, ed. and trans. H. T. Riley (1868), p. 426, quoted G. G. Coulton, *op. cit.*, p. 327

The Ordinance of the Cooks, ordered by the Mayor and Aldermen, as to divers flesh-meat and poultry, as well roasted as baked in pasties:

The best roast pig, for 8d. Best roast goose, 7d. Best roast capon, 6d. Best roast hen, 4d. Best roast pullet, 2½d. Best roast rabbit, 4d. Best roast river mallard, 4½d. Best roast dunghill mallard, 3½d. Best roast teal, 2½d. Best roast snipe, 1½d. Five roast larks, 1½d. Best roast woodcock, 2½d. Best roast partridge, 3½d. Best roast plover, 2½d. Best roast pheasant, 13d. Best roast curlew, 6½d. Three roast thrushes, 2d. Ten roast finches, 1d. Best roast heron, 18d. Best roast bittern, 20d. Three roast pigeons, 2½d. Ten eggs, one penny. For the paste, fire, and trouble upon a capon, 1½d. For the paste, fire, and trouble upon a goose, 2d. The best capon baked in a pasty, 8d. The best hen baked in a pasty, 5d. The best lamb, roasted, 7d.

❧

Villein Services in the Thirteenth Century

Source: Holkham Deed 4

Hervey de Monte holds 18 acres for 22d. rent at 4 times of payment and 4 hens worth 4d. and does 3 half days weeding worth ½d. and 3 boon-works in Autumn at the lord's board worth 6d. and does 1 boon-work with a plough, if he has a horse, worth 6d.

at the lord's board and gives 2d. for Wodelode and carries the writ of the king twice a year worth 4d. and if the lord comes to the vill he lends him a horse if he has one to carry bread for 12 leagues and goes twice to the lord's mill pond worth 1d. twice a year and pays ½d. for Wardsea and carried the lord's corn in Autumn for one day worth 2d. if he has a horse. Total 4s. 1d. . . .

Roger Haven and Hervey Carpenter hold 32 acres for 26d. and fold service 9d. and 2 quarters of oats worth 2s. and make 2 quarters of malt at the lord's board worth 3d. and will carry half a measure of dung worth 4½d. and 16 works in Autumn and 3 boon-works in Autumn worth 19d. and will thrash for 32 days worth 16d. and 2 boon-works with a plough worth 12d. if they have horses at the lord's board and will weed for 3 half days worth 1½d. and will do a carrying duty worth 3d. and will go to the pond 4 times worth 2d. and pay 4 hens worth 4d. and will carry in Autumn if they have a horse at the lord's board worth 6d. Total 10s. 10d. . . .

❖

Farming Duties in the Thirteenth Century

Source: Fleta, quoted F. H. Cripps-Day, *The Manor Farm* (1931), pp. 76–7

CONCERNING PLOUGHMEN

The art of the ploughmen consists in knowing how to draw a straight furrow with yoked oxen without striking, pricking or ill-treating them.

Ploughmen ought not to be melancholy, or irritable, but gay, full of song and joyous, so that they may in a sort of way encourage the oxen at their toil with melody and song; they must take them their forage and fodder, and they ought to be attached to them, and sleep in their stable at night, and make much of them, curry and rub them down, look after them well in every way taking care that their forage and fodder is not stolen; the allowance of hay or litter should not be given out for two or three nights at once, but as much as is required for a day's feed should be given to them every day, nor should they be permitted to have a candle unless, as the saying is, it is 'held' [i.e. a lantern].

Other people's beasts found in the ploughmen's pasture ought to be impounded. It is the duty of the ploughmen and husbandmen when the tillage season is over, to ditch, thresh, dig, fence, repair the watercourses in the fields, and to do other such small and useful tasks.

CONCERNING SHEPHERDS

Shepherds should be intelligent, watchful, and kind men who will not harry the sheep by their bad temper, but let them graze peacefully and without disturbing them.

Let each provide himself with a good barking dog and sleep out every night with his flock. Let him prepare his folds and sheepcotes and provide good hurdles covered with pelts and thick rushes for warmth; and he must be careful that the sheep in his charge are not stolen or changed, nor allowed to graze in wet or marshy places, in thickets, or on low-lying bottoms, or on unhealthy pastures, lest, for want of good care, they go sick and die, otherwise he will be held liable for the penalty of the account.

But let there be three folds for the sheep and their lambs, viz, one for the muttons and wethers, another for the two-tooth ewes and a third for hogs of one year and under, if the flock is large enough, three shepherds must then be put in charge.

All the sheep must be marked with the same mark. The ewes should not be allowed to be suckled or milked beyond the feast of the Nativity of the Blessed Mary [8 Sept.]; those which it is not expedient to keep should be drafted out between Easter and Whitsuntide, sheared earlier, marked differently from the others, and be sent at once into the wood pastures where they should be kept, or in some other pasture in which they will fatten and improve more rapidly; they may be sold at the feast of the Nativity of St John the Baptist [24 June].

Those that are sickly can be recognised by the teeth dropping out and by the sign of old age; the wool of these may be sold with the pelts of those dying of murrain; and hence much may be saved on these by shrewdness, for some careful people have the flesh of those dying of murrain put into water for the period between the hour of nine and vespers, and afterwards hung up so that the water drains off; the flesh is afterwards salted and dried and they are made worth something and can be distributed among the workpeople and the household; and to prevent loss in the account an allowance in the daily expenses according to a fixed price can be made for the flesh so used. . . .

❖

A Manor in 1307

Source: Custumals of Battle Abbey, trans. D. C. Munro (1934), pp. 94–8

Extent of the manor of Bernehorne, made on Wednesday following the feast of St. Gregory the pope, in the thirty-fifth year of the reign of King Edward, in the presence of Brother Thomas, keeper of Marley, John de la More, and Adam de Thrughlegh, clerks, on the oath of William de Gocecoumbe, Walter le Parker, Richard le Knyst, Richard the son of the latter, Andrew of Estone, Stephen Morsprich, Thomas Brembel, William of Swynham, John Pollard, Roger le Glide, John Syward, and John de Lillingewist, who say that there are all the following holdings:

The total of the acres of woods is 12 acres.

The total of the acres of arable land is 444 acres and 3 roods, of which 147 acres 4 roods are maritime land, 101 acres marshy land, and 180 acres waste ground.

The total of the acres of meadow is 13 acres 1 rood.

The total of the whole preceding extent £18. 10s. 4d.

John Pollard holds a half acre in Aldithewisse and owes 18d. at the four terms, and owes from it relief and heriot.

John Suthington holds a house and 40 acres of land and owes 3s. 6d. at Easter and Michaelmas.

William of Swynhamme holds 1 acre of meadow in the thicket of Swynhamme and owes 1d. at the feast of Michaelmas.

Ralph of Leybourne holds a cottage and 1 acre of land in Pinden and owes 3s. at Easter and Michaelmas, and attendance at the court in the manor every three weeks, relief and heriot.

Richard Knyst of Swynham holds two acres and a half of land and owes yearly 4s.

William at Knelle holds 2 acres of land in Aldithewisse and owes yearly 4s.

Roger le Glede holds a cottage and 3 roods of land and owes 2s. 6d. at Easter and Michaelmas.

Alexander Hamound holds a little piece of land near Aldithewisse and owes 1 goose, of the value of 2d.

The sum of the whole rent of the free tenants, with the value of the goose, is 18s. 9d.

They say moreover than John of Cayworth holds a house and 30 acres of land, and owes yearly 2s. at Easter and Michaelmas; and he owes a cock and two hens at Christmas, of the value of 4d.

And he ought to harrow for two days at the Lenten sowing with one man and his own horse and his own barrow, the value of the work being 4d., and he is to receive from the lord on each day 3 meals, of the value of 5d., and then the lord will be at a loss of 1d. Thus his harrowing is of no value to the service of the lord.

And he ought to carry the manure of the lord for 2 days with 1 cart, with his own 2 oxen, the value of the work being 8d., and he is to receive from the lord each day 3 meals of the price as above. And thus the service is worth 3d. clear.

And he shall find 1 man for 2 days for mowing the meadow of the lord, who can mow, by estimation 1 acre and a half, the value of the mowing of an acre being 6d., the sum is therefore 9d., and he is to receive each day 3 meals of the value given above; and thus that mowing is worth 4d. clear.

And he ought to gather and carry that same hay which he has cut, the price of the work being 3d.

And he shall have from the lord 2 meals for 1 man, of the value of 1½d. Thus the work will be worth 1½d. clear.

And he ought to carry the hay of the lord for 1 day with a cart and 3 animals of his own, the price of the work being 6d. And he shall have from the lord 3 meals of the value of 2½d. And thus the work is worth 3½d. clear.

And he ought to carry in autumn beans or oats for 2 days with a cart and 3 animals of his own, the value of the work being 12d. And he shall receive from the lord each day 3 meals of the value given above; and thus the work is worth 7d. clear.

And he ought to find 1 man for 2 days to cut heath, the value of the work being 4d. and he shall have 3 meals each day of the value given above; and thus the lord will lose if he receives the service, 3d. Thus that mowing is worth nothing to the service of the lord.

And he ought to carry the heath which he has cut, the value of the work being 5d. And he shall receive from the lord 3 meals at the price of 2½d. And thus the work will be worth 2½d. clear.

And he ought to carry to Battle, twice in the summer season, each time half a load of grain, the value of the service being 4d. And he shall receive in the manor each time 1 meal of the value of 2d. And thus the work is worth 2d. clear.

The totals of the rents, with the value of the hens, is 2s. 4d.

The total value of the works is 2s. 3½d., owed from the said John yearly.

William of Cayworth holds a house and 30 acres of land and owes at Easter and Michaelmas 2s. rent. And he shall do all customs just as the aforesaid John of Cayworth.

William atte Grene holds a house and 30 acres of land and owes in all things the same as the said John.

Alan atte Felde holds a house and 16 acres of land (for which the sergeant pays to the court of Bixley 2s.), and he owes at Easter and Michaelmas 4s., attendance at the manor court, relief and heriot.

John Lyllingwyst holds a house and 4 acres of land and owes at the two terms 2s., attendance at the manor court, relief and heriot.

The same John holds 1 acre of land in the fields of Hoo and owes at the two periods 2s. attendance, relief, and heriot.

Reginald atte Denne holds a house and 18 acres of land and owes at the same periods 18d., attendance, relief, and heriot.

Robert of Northehou holds 3 acres of land at Saltcoat and owes at the said periods attendance, relief and heriot.

Total of the rents of the villeins, with the value of the hens, 20s.

Total of all the works of these three villeins, 6s. 10½d.

And it is to be noted that none of the above-named villeins can give their daughters in marriage, nor cause their sons to be tonsured, nor can they cut down timber growing on the lands they hold, without licence of the bailiff or sergeant of the lord, and then for building purposes and not otherwise. And after the death of any one of the aforesaid villeins, the lord shall have as a heriot his best animal if he had any; if, however, he had no living beast, the lord shall have no heriot, as they say. The sons or daughters of the aforesaid villeins shall give, for entrance into the holding after the death of their predecessors, as much as they give of rent per year.

Sylvester, the priest, holds 1 acre of meadow adjacent to his house and owes yearly 3s.

Total of the rents of tenants for life, 3s.

Petronilla atte Holme holds a cottage and a piece of land and owes at Easter and Michaelmas . . .; also attendance, relief, and heriot.

Walter Herying holds a cottage and a piece of land and owes at Easter and Michaelmas 18d., attendance, relief, and heriot.

Isabella Mariner holds a cottage and owes at the feast of St. Michael 12d., attendance, relief, and heriot.

Jordan atte Melle holds a cottage and 1½ acres of land and owes at Easter and Michaelmas 2s., attendance, relief, and heriot.

William of Batelesmere holds 1 acre of land with a cottage and owes at the feast of St. Michael 3d., and 1 cock and 1 hen at Christmas of the value of 3d., attendance, relief and heriot.

John le Man holds half an acre of land with a cottage and owes at the feast of St. Michael 2s., attendance, relief, and heriot.

John Werthe holds 1 rood of land with a cottage and owes at the said term 18d., attendance, relief and heriot.

Geoffrey Caumbreis holds half an acre and a cottage and owes at the said term 18d., attendance, relief, and heriot.

William Hassok holds 1 rood of land and a cottage and owes at the said term 18d., attendance, relief, and heriot.

The same man holds 3½ acres of land and owes yearly at the feast of St. Michael 3s. for all.

Roger Doget holds half an acre of land and a cottage, which were those of R. the miller, and owes at the fast of St. Michael 18d., attendance, relief, and heriot.

Thomas le Brod holds 1 acre and a cottage and owes at the said term 3s., attendance, relief, and heriot.

Agnes of Cayworth holds half an acre and a cottage and owes at the said term 8d., attendance, relief and heriot. . . .

Total of the rents of the said cottages, with the value of the hens, 34s. 6d.

And it is to be noted that all the said cottagers shall do as regards giving their daughters in marriage, having their sons tonsured, cutting down timber, paying heriot, and giving fines for entrance, just as John of Cayworth and the rest of the villeins above mentioned.

Note: Fines and penalties, with heriots and reliefs, are worth yearly 5s.

❖

The Black Death (1348)

Source: Henry Knighton, *Readings in English Social History*, ed. R. B. Morgan (1923) pp. 145-7

The grievous plague penetrated the sea coasts from Southampton and came to Bristol, and there almost the whole strength of the town died, struck as it were by sudden death; for there were few who kept their beds more than three days, or two days, or half a day; and after this the fell death broke forth on every side with the course of the sun. There died at Leicester in the small parish of St. Leonard more than 380; and in the parish of the Holy Cross more than 400; and so in each parish a great number. . . . In the same year there was a great plague of sheep everywhere in the realm, so that in one place there died in one pasturage more than 5,000 sheep, and so rotted that neither beast nor bird would touch them. And there were smaller prices for everything on account of the fear of death. For there were very few who cared about riches or anything else. For a man could have a house which before was worth 40s. for 6s. 8d., a fat ox for 4s., a cow for 12d., a heifer for 6d., a fat wether for 4d., a sheep for 8d., a lamb for 2d., a big pig for 5d., a stone of wool for 9d. Sheep and cattle went wandering over fields and through crops and there was no one to go and drive or father them, so that the number cannot be reckoned which perished in the ditches in every district for lack of herdsmen; for there was such a lack of servants that no one knew what he ought to do.

In the following autumn no one could get a reaper for less than 8d. with his food, a mower for less than 12d. with his food. Wherefore, many crops perished in the fields for want of someone to gather them; but in the pestilence year, as is above said of other things, there was such abundance of all kinds of corn that no one much troubled about it.

. . . Priests were in such poverty that many churches were widowed and lacking the divine offices, masses, matins, vespers, sacraments, and other rites . . . but within a short time a very great multitude of those whose wives had died in the pestilence flocked into orders, of whom many were illiterate and little more than lay-men, except so far as they knew how to read, although they could not understand.

Meanwhile the King sent proclamation into all the counties that reapers and other labourers should not take more than they had been accustomed to take under the penalty appointed by statute. But the labourers were so lifted up and obstinate that they would not listen to the King's command, but if any wished to have them he had to give them what they wanted, and either lose his fruit and

crops or satisfy the lofty and covetous desires of the workmen . . .
after the aforesaid pestilence many buildings, great and small, fell
into ruins in every city, borough and village for lack of inhabitants,
likewise many villages and hamlets became desolate, all having died
who dwelt there.

❖

An Ordinance Concerning Labourers and Servants (1349)

Source: Statutes of the Realm (1810–28), Vol. I p. 307, trans. C.
Stephenson and F. G. Marcham *op. cit.*, p. 225

The king to the sheriff of Kent, Greeting. Because a great part of
the people, and especially of workmen and servants, late died of the
pestilence, many seeing the necessity of masters, and great scarcity
of servants, will not serve unless they may receive excessive wages,
and some rather willing to beg in idleness, than by labour to get
their living; we, considering the grievous incommodities, which of
the lack especially of ploughmen and such labourers may hereafter
come, have upon deliberation and treaty with the prelates and the
nobles, and learned men assisting us, of their mutual consent
ordained:

1. That every man and woman of our realm of England, of what
condition he be, free or bond, able in body, and within the age of
three score years, not living in merchandise, nor exercising any
craft, nor having of his own whereof he may live, nor proper land,
about whose tillage he may himself occupy, and not serving any
other, if he be required to serve in convenient service, his estate
considered, he shall be bounden to serve him which shall so him
require; and take only the wages, livery, meed, or salary, which
were accustomed to be given in the places where he oweth to serve,

the twentieth year of our reign in England, or five or six other common years next before. Provided always, that the lords be preferred before others in their bondmen or their land tenants, so in their service to be retained: so that nevertheless the said lords shall retain no more than shall be necessary for them; and if any such man or woman, being so required to serve, will not do the same, that proved by two true men before the sheriff, bailiff, lord, or constable of the town where the same shall happen to be done, he shall anon be taken by them, or any of them, and committed to the next jail, there to remain under strait keeping, till he find surety to serve in the form aforesaid.

. . . .

5. Item, that sadlers, skinners, whitetawers, cordwainers, tailors, smiths, carpenters, masons, tilers, boatmen, carters, and all other artificers and workmen, shall not take for their labour and workmanship above the same that was wont to be paid to such persons the said twentieth year, and other common years next before, as afore is said, in the place where they shall happen to work; and if any man take more, he shall be committed to the next jail, in manner as afore is said.

6. Item, that butchers, fishmongers, hostelers, brewers, bakers, pulters, and all other sellers of all manner of victual, shall be bound to sell the same victual for a reasonable price, having respect to the price that such victual be sold at in the places adjoining, so that the same sellers have moderate gains, and not excessive, reasonably to be required according to the distance of the place from whence the said victuals be carried; . . .

The Peasants' Revolt at St. Albans (1381)

Source: Thomas Walsingham, *English History*, trans. R. B. Morgan, *Readings in English Social History* (1923), pp. 189–96

Appalling threats forced all to rally regardless of ploughing and sowing . . . some lads had sticks, others rusty swords, axes, or smoke-stained bows . . . they slew lawyers old and young . . . and decided to burn all court rolls and old muniments. . . . During Matins on Friday [14 June, 1381] hasty messengers from Barnet to St. Albans said the Commons bade speed to London with the Barnet and St. Albans men with their best arms, or else 20,000 would burn the vills and coerce them. Informed at once, the abbot dreaded the damage of such a raid and quickly summoned the servants and villeins of his court to bid them speed to London to appease and stop them. So they hurried off enthusiastically. They found a mob of 2000 yokels burning the valuable farm of the Hospitallers at Highbury and busy pulling down the ruins. The ringleader John [Jack] Straw made them swear loyalty to 'King Richard and the Commons'. Other mobs were at Mile End and at Tower Hill where they killed Archbishop Sudbury, who worked miracles posthumously. Richard II gave them charters dated 15 June granting freedom to the serfs of various counties.

On reaching London the Abbey villeins and servants separated. The former in St. Mary Arches church debated services to the Abbey and how to achieve ancient aspirations, like new town boundaries, free pastures and fisheries, revival of lost sporting rights, freedom to establish hand mills, the exclusion of the liberty's bailiff from the town limits, and the return of bonds made by their sires to the late abbot Richard of Wallingford. . . .

They decided both to hurry home with authority from [Wat] Tyler, the Kentish vagabond king, making demands with threats of fire and slaughter, and to extort an order under royal privy seal to the abbot to restore their rights as in Henry's reign. William Gryndecobbe, the biggest debtor of the monastery, reared there, a neighbour and relation of the monks, was so forward in the business that the mob saw him kneel to the king six times to get that order, and he was chief spokesman with Walter, the rustic idol. Walter did not want to leave London or send a party but Gryndecobbe and other rascals swore loyalty to him so he promised to come with 20,000 if necessary to shave the beards of abbot, prior and monks [i.e. to behead them]. An abbey servant got home before them by a dashing ride to say the treasurer and many others were murdered, the Commons were merciless executioners and the prior would be beheaded and the other monks imperilled if they stayed. The prior, four monks and various associates fled on horse and on foot the dangerous trail to Tynemouth. Soon the villeins were back, led by William Gryndecobbe and William Cadyndon, baker, who coveted some obvious success before their comrades arrived, longing to get extra credit so as to seem important afterwards. They reported good progress. They would be masters not slaves, and that very night they would break the abbot's folds in Falcon and other woods and demolish the gates of Eye and other woods with the sub-cellarer's house, opposite the street where fish was sold, as it spoilt the townsman's view and damaged prestige. The fools took rapid action. . . . Thus ended Friday at St. Albans with its train of evil.

On Saturday morning [15 June] the St. Albans men arose to review their crimes. A monster procession marched to Falcon wood, calling out all of military age on pain of death or destruction of their house or goods; threats united the decent and criminal. Our William Gryndecobbe and William Cadyndon led. At the rendez-vous the mob plotted its demands, actions and threats. They decided to finish off the folds and coppice gates, and did so. Back in town they awaited peasants from surrounding villages and the home farm. They had summoned with menaces 2000 or more rascals to rally about freedom from St. Albans. They would gain any demands and not let any gentlemen linger at home but bring them as supporters. From Wat Tyler they learnt the trick of executing the hesitant or wrecking their homes.

The sight of the mob they had conjured up raised their spirits, clasping hands and swearing oaths. An arrogant rush to the abbey gates showed Walter's power. The gates were opened and they contemptuously told the porter to open the prison. Some godly villeins had told the abbot and he had told the porter the plan, so he obeyed. They freed the captives in return for unswerving support except for one whom they judged and butchered in the space before the gate, yelling diabolically as they had learnt at the archbishop's murder in London and setting the head on the pillory. Soon allies from Barnet arrived and Richard de Wallingford, a substantial St. Albans villein, briskly rode up from London with the royal letter Gryndecobbe had kept demanding, bearing the banner of St. George like the criminals in London.

They swarmed round him as he dismounted and planted his standard where they should stand until he brought the abbot's answer. The leaders entered the church with him and sent word to the abbot's chamber to answer the Commons. The monks convinced the abbot that the death which he would have preferred would not save the abbey's rights so he went down to them like a beaten man. Wallingford showed him the letter extracted from the king by Gryndecobbe dated 15 June about certain charters from King Henry concerning common, pasture and fishing rights. The abbot raised legal objections but Wallingford said the Commons did not expect excuses, would turn on him if kept waiting, and would summon Wat Tyler and 20,000 men. The abbot complained that he had befriended them for 32 years. Admitting this, they said they had hoped to get their demands from his successor. He yielded everything to the lesser evil. They burnt many charters by the market cross and also demanded a certain old charter about the liberties of the villeins 'with gold and blue capital letters'. He said he had never seen this but would hunt for it. The leaders reported a promise of a new charter, and the rascals went into the cloister with the deeds and ripped up millstones set in the parlour floor to commemorate an old suit between the villeins and the late abbot Richard. Smashing these, they distributed fragments like holy bread in a parish church. Meal time was granted and allowed sad reflection on slaves become masters and life and death in the hands of merciless countrymen. London had lain at their will a day and a night, the archbishop and treasurer were executed, the king was captive, his soldiery power-less. . . .

At the ninth hour the villeins came back for their charter, or else 2000 of them would destroy the gate. The abbot prepared a charter to be read and then sealed, but they sent a squire for clerk with ink and parchment to write at their dictation. They insisted that there was another charter of old liberties which they would have or wreck the abbey. He offered to swear at the morrow's mass that he with-held nothing, but they scorned his oaths, keener to destroy the abbey than get charters. Ale and a great basket of bread were put at the gate for all as a sop, which did not work, until the chief towns-men risked telling them to be quiet. They then left the gate to join another mob sacking houses on Walter's London pattern.

Under the royal colours they dared to set watches round the town against any help and to execute any monks going in or out. On the morrow they invited any with financial claims on the abbey to appear, and one demanded 100 marks damages, threatening to burn St. Peter's Grange and Kyngebury manor, which he had leased until he fled for debt. He had 2000 Commons near to avenge his wrongs and would rather make payment on the prior's body than recover his cash.

The monks had a sleepless night because of the impossible demand of the villeins to produce the unfindable charter, but Sunday [16 June] brought hopeful rumours of Tyler's death and London's rally to the king. A royal messenger enjoined peace, bringing a letter of royal protection for the abbey. Mobs summoned from Luton, Watford, Barnet, Rickmansworth and Tring arrived and the townsmen did not wish to seem disheartened or obedient to the king. Regardless of the future they would get their charters, but with a more conciliatory air. . . . The chief townsmen entered the abbot's chamber, stood over the clerk, inserting their requirements about liberties in the charter, and made the abbot seal a bond in £1000 to produce the non-existent charter, if found. Sir Hugh Segrave, royal steward, and Thomas Percy wrote advising every concession as it would never be held valid, so the abbot gave his bond. They acted as lords, not servants, in the abbot's chamber and chapel, present at the engrossing, dictating words and superintending the sealing. The seal which showed St. Alban holding a palm was properly applied to their charter but miraculously it thrice stuck to the wax to show that the martyr did not want them for masters but would keep his lordship over them. They departed gleefully to publish the new charter at the cross with the royal pardon and manumission. They even published the royal charter of protection to show goodwill, but with malice at heart as appears.

On Monday and Tuesday villeins from all the abbey's vills came urgently requiring charters of manumission pursuant to the royal charter. These were made in a standard form. Then the villagers thought themselves gentry of royal blood who need not even pay rent. . . . They made grammar school masters swear never to teach boys grammar. . . . They tried to burn all records and killed all who could record past or current events. It was dangerous to be known as a clerk and worse still to be found carrying an inkhorn. . . .

The abbot then sent some villeins to swell the royal army, but they claimed to have come on their own authority. Richard Peeres recognised some as ringleaders at St. Albans, imprisoned them and would have executed them—on the vigil of the passion of St. Alban, the eighth day after the Friday. During matins the chief townsmen went to enlist the abbot's help. In distress he despatched a monk to London to see the prisoners released, which he did. . . .

The king proposed to come to do justice at St. Albans, but Sir Walter Atte Lee, a local man, feared the damage done by such a host and persuaded the king to commission him to make peace between villeins and abbot. William Gryndecobbe persuaded them not to bolt but to meet him and if he did not come as a friend to drive him away. They greeted him and he made the people collect in the shape of a rainbow, while he with his armed guard about him explained that he came with a commission to prevent the damage threatened by the proposed arrival of the royal army. He adjured them to give up the ringleaders and make peace with the abbey. Some applauded but the jury said nobody should be indicted. When told to give up the charters they prevaricated, alleging intimidation, and ignorance as to who held them. The abbot said he trusted their consciences and mollified the knight by saying he needed no intermediary. The knight called a meeting at Barnet Wood but did little for fear of the villeins there—about 300 stood round with bows, especially Barnet and Berkhamstead men, and if he had tried to do justice they would probably have made a riot and his soldiers have joined them. He secretly told the bailiffs and constables, when the mob dispersed, to compass the capture of William Gryndecobbe, William Cadyndon, John the barber who had removed the millstones from the pavement, with other notorieties. He hastened to Hertford whither he wanted them brought. Richard Peeres, John Chival, Thomas Eydon and William Eccleshale, admirable squires of the abbot, captured the three with the unwilling help of the bailiffs and put them in the gate. Next morning they were taken to Hertford with the chief townsmen of St. Albans and all the abbot's squires and varlets to reinforce the knight in doing justice. On their departure the town seethed with hot air and empty oaths—a hundred would die if one neighbour fell. Mobs gathered in fields and woods outside the town and, with the defenders away, the abbey looked like getting burnt, so the abbot in alarm summoned some local gentry for protection. Hearing his squires were gone executing the prisoners he wrote for them to hurry back to dispel this new danger. The trial was on and they grieved to go for otherwise they would have seen them executed, but they hurried home. . . . Two stopped in gaol but William Gryndecobbe was released, on three neighbours going bail for £300 each, to return to prison next Saturday.

The villeins wavered between violence and conciliation, now incited by Gryndecobbe, now depressed by the reported approach of the Earl of Warwick and Thomas Percy, now elated by the diversion of Warwick, now dismayed by the approach of the king himself. The abbot asked Hugh Segrave in London to divert the king because of the damage threatened by the royal entourage to crops, though the villeins alleged that the abbot spent £1,000 to ruin them. They hired an expensive lawyer to compromise with the abbot, repairing damage, replacing as many millstones as were removed, and returning extorted charters. The abbot met the king at the west gate with bells ringing. He had thousands of tenants in chief, soldiers and Robert Tresilian the justiciar. The ringleaders were kept prisoner until Monday while John Ball was brought to St. Albans tried [14 July] and hanged [15 July]. . . .

The jury refused to indict, but Tresilian produced a list of ring-leaders, forcing the jury to indict and getting assent from second and third juries. William Gryndecobbe, William Cadyndon, John the barber and other criminals to the number of 15 were drawn and hanged for riot. Some leading townsmen like Richard, John Garlick, William Berewill and Thomas the Stink, were imprisoned, with 80 others whom royal clemency later released. Meanwhile the villeins spitefully accused the abbot, who had risked royal displeasure by his intercessions, of forcing them to join the London mob. Such malice shocked the justiciar who silenced them by asking why the abbot did so. Other slanders about the abbot's reduction of freemen to villeinage, compulsion to use his mill instead of grinding at home, and bribing the king were shaking most of the abbey's friends, despite penalties for slander, against the abbot, of hanging for men and burning for women. After 8 days the king met the obvious perversity of the abbey's dependents by sending a commission to see that the abbey's dues were rendered—for the royal chancery was being held in the chapter-house so that the abbot could manage things better.

On St. Margaret's Day after eating, the king was to go to Berkhampstead Castle. In the great abbey hall he first took an oath of fealty from the men of Hertfordshire between 15 and 60 years old. They swore to prefer death to obedience to agitators, to seize agitators and render their dues . . . the king was amazed to hear that the bodies of those hanged at St. Albans had been audaciously taken from the gallows so he sent a writ dated 3 August to the bailiffs, bidding them be replaced in chains to hang as long as they lasted. This reduced to a revolting slavery the freedom-loving revolutionaries of St. Albans, for none would do the work for them and with their own hands they had to hang up their fellow citizens whose decomposing bodies were full of maggots and stank. It was just for men who usurped the name 'citizen' to have the disgusting task whereby they earned the apt name of 'hangmen' to their lasting shame. . . .

Enclosures

Source: Polydore Vergil, *English History*, quoted J. J. Bagley, *Historical Interpretation* (1965), p. 239

For half a century or more previously, the sheep-farming nobles had tried to find devices whereby they might increase the annual income of their lands. As a result the yeomen had incurred very considerable losses. The sheep farmers, cultivating pasturage (after the manner of Arabs) rather than arable, began everywhere to employ far fewer agricultural labourers, to destroy rural dwelling-houses, to create vast deserts, to allow the land to waste while filling it up with herds, flocks and a multitude of beasts; in like fashion they fenced off all these pastures to keep them private, thus establishing in their own right a monopoly of wool, sheep and cattle. From this three evil consequences ensued for the state. First, the number of peasants, upon whom the prince chiefly relies for waging war, was reduced. Second, a larger number of villages and towns, many stripped of inhabitants, were ruined. Third, the wool and cloth which was then produced, as well as the flesh of all kinds of animals which is fit for human consumption began to sell much more dearly than it used to do, so that the price has not really dropped even to this day. . . .

Building by Henry III

Source: L. F. Salzmann, *Building in England down to* 1540 (1952), p. 384

1249 Woodstock

Orders to crenellate the queen's chamber with freestone, and to raise the chimney of that chamber to the height of 8 feet; to panel the lower chamber and make the privy chamber in the fashion of that chamber where Bartholomew Pecche used to sleep; to build a chamber at the gateway of Evereswell, 40 feet long and 22 feet wide, with a wardrobe, privy chamber, and fireplace. Also to repair Rosamund's chamber, unroofed by the wind; and to make a door to the queen's chamber, and a door to the old larder. Also to repair the bays of both our fish-stews and the causeway of the lower stew near the enclosure; to put 2 windows of white glass in the gable of the hall, and 2 in the chamber of Edward our son, and 2 windows barred with iron in the old larder. To make leaden spouts round the alures [walks] of the same Edward's chamber; to repair all the buildings of each court where necessary; to bar the windows of the porch with iron; to build a house for our napery; and to pull down the rooms of William our chaplain and rebuild them between the hall and the queen's stable, making a garden on the site of the said rooms.

1250 Westminster Abbey

Relaxation for one year's enjoined penance to penitents who assist the fabric of the church of wonderful beauty now being built by the King at Westminster.

1250 Clarendon

Orders to make a baptistry in the chapel of All Saints there, and to put on the chapel a bell-turret with two bells, and to make a crucifix with two images on each side of wood, and an image of Blessed Mary with her Child. And let the queen's chamber be decently paved. And in the queen's hall let there be made a window towards the garden, well barred with iron; and two windows in the queen's chapel, one on each side of the altar, which are to be divided down the middle so that they may be opened and shut when necessary. . . . And make a bench round our great garden beside the wall, and whitewash the wall above it. In Alexander's chamber let there be made a wardrobe with a privy chamber, and roof those buildings well. Make a garden below our chamber on the north; also a window in our wardrobe; and lengthen our chandlery by four or five couples.

✦

Building the Octagon at Ely Cathedral

Source: Historia Eliensis, H. Wharton, *Anglia Sacra* (1691), Vol. I pp. 643–4, trans. G. G. Coulton, *op. cit.,* pp. 480–1

[One night] when the brethren had made their procession to the shrines in honour of St. Ermengilda, and were returning to the dormitory, scarce had one or two lain down upon their beds when, behold! the central tower suddenly fell and overwhelmed the choir, with such a crash and din that men might have thought it an earthquake; yet no man was hurt or crushed by its fall. . . . Alan [de Walsingham], our Sacrist, was sore grieved and afflicted at this most baleful and lamentable chance, not knowing whither to turn, or what possible means could be found of repairing so vast a ruin. But, plucking up courage, and putting all his trust in the help of God and of His most gracious Mother, and in the merits of the holy virgin Ethelreda, he put out his hand to strong things. First, he spent great labour and much money in removing from the Cathedral the fallen stones and beams; then he purged the holy building with all possible haste from the masses of dust which lay there. Finally he measured out in eight divisions, with the art of an architect, the place where he thought to build the new tower; and he set the workmen to dig and search for the foundations of the eight stone columns where-upon the whole building should be supported, and beneath which the choir with its stalls might afterwards be built; until at last he found solid and secure ground for all this under-structure. Then, when these eight places had been carefully dug out and firmly founded with stones and sand, at last he began those eight columns, with the stonework which they supported. This he completed in six years, bringing it up to the upper string-course in the year of our Lord 1328. Then, without delay, that cunningly-wrought timber structure of the new tower was begun; a structure designed with the utmost and most marvellous subtlety of human thought, to be set upon the aforesaid stonework. This in its turn was completed, with vast and burdensome expense, especially in seeking far and wide for the great beams which were needed to support this building, which were found at last with the utmost difficulty and at great cost, and which were brought by land or sea to Ely. These beams were carved and shaped by skilful workmen, and bound together into the fabric with marvellous art; thus at length, with God's help, the tower was brought to that honourable consummation which had long been desired. The whole cost of this new tower, during the twenty years of Alan de Walsingham's time, was £2,400. 6s. 11d., whereof £206. 1s. came from gifts.

❖

The Wedding of Henry III (1236)

Source: Matthew Paris, *English History*, trans. J. A. Giles (1852–4), Vol. I pp. 8–9

There were assembled at the king's nuptial festivities such a host of nobles of both sexes, such numbers of religious men, such crowds of the populace, and such a variety of actors, that London, with its capacious bosom, could scarcely contain them. The whole city was ornamented with flags and banners, chaplets and hangings, candles and lamps, and with wonderful devices and extraordinary representations, and all the roads were cleansed from mud and dirt, sticks, and everything offensive. The citizens too, went out to meet the king and queen, dressed out in their ornaments, and vied with each other in trying the speed of their horses. On the same day, when they left the city for Westminster, to perform the duties of butler to the king (which office belonged to them by right of old, at the coronation), they proceeded thither dressed in silk garments, with mantles worked in gold, and with costly changes of raiment, mounted on valuable horses, glittering with new bits and saddles, and riding in troops arranged in order. They carried with them three hundred and sixty gold and silver cups, preceded by the king's trumpeters and with horns sounding, so that such a wonderful novelty struck all who beheld it with astonishment. The Archbishop of Canterbury, by the right especially belonging to him, performed the duty of crowning, with the usual solemnities, the Bishop of London assisting him as a dean, the other bishops taking their stations according to their rank. In the same way all the abbots, at the head of whom, as was his right, was the Abbot of St. Albans (for as the Protomartyr of England Blessed Alban was the chief of all the martyrs of England, so also was his abbot the chief of all the abbots in rank and dignity), as the authentic privileges of that church set forth. The nobles, too, performed the duties, which, by ancient right and custom, pertained to them at the coronations of kings. In like manner some of the inhabitants of certain cities discharged certain duties which belonged to them by right of their ancestors. The Earl of Chester carried the sword of St. Edward, which was called 'Curtein', before the king, as a sign that he was earl of the palace, and had by right the power of restraining the king if he should commit an error. The earl was attended by the Constable of Chester, who kept the people away with a wand when they pressed forward in a disorderly way. The grand marshal of England, the Earl of Pembroke, carried a wand before the king and cleared the way before him both in the church and in the banquet-hall, and arranged the banquet and the guests at table. The Wardens of the Cinque Ports carried the pall over the king, supported by four spears, but the claim to this duty was not altogether undisputed. The Earl of Leicester supplied the king with water in basins to wash before his meal; the Earl of Warenne performed the duty of king's cupbearer, supplying the place of the Earl of Arundel, because the latter was a youth and not as yet made a belted knight. Master Michael Belet was butler ex officio, the Earl of Hereford performed the duties of marshal of the king's household, and William Beauchamp held the station of almoner. The justiciary of the forests arranged the drinking cups on the table at the king's right hand although he met with some opposition, which however fell to the ground. The citizens of London passed the wine about in all directions, in costly cups, and those of Winchester superintended the cooking of the feast; the rest, according to the ancient statutes, filled their separate stations, or made their claims to do so. And in order that the nuptial festivities might not be clouded by any disputes, saving the right of anyone, many things were put up with for the time which they left for decision at a more favourable opportunity. The office of Chancellor of England, and all the offices connected with the king, are ordained and assized in the Exchequer. Therefore the chancellor, the chamberlain, the marshal, and the constable, by right of their office, took their seats there, as also did the barons, according to the date of their creation, in the city of London, whereby they each knew his own place. The ceremony was splendid, with the gay dresses of the clergy and knights who were present. The Abbot of Westminster sprinkled the holy water, and the treasurer, acting the part of sub-dean, carried the paten. Why should I describe all those persons who reverently ministered in the church of God as was their duty? Why describe the abundance of meats and dishes on the table? the quantity of venison, the variety of fish, the joyous sounds of the glee-men, and the gaiety of the waiters? Whatever the world could afford to create pleasure and magnificence was there brought together from every quarter.

❖

The Coronation of Henry IV
(1399)

Source: Froissart, *Chronicles,* trans. Thomas Johnes (1803–5), ed. H. P. Dunham (1906), pp. 611–14

On Tuesday, the last day of September, 1399, a parliament was held at Westminster, at which the Duke of Lancaster challenged the crown of England, and claimed it for his own, for three reasons— first, by conquest; second, from being heir to it; and third, from the pure and free resignation which King Richard had made of it. The Parliament then declared, that it was their will he should be king, and the day of coronation was fixed for the feast of Saint Edward, which fell on a Monday, the 13th day of October.

On Saturday before the coronation, the new king went from Westminster to the Tower of London, attended by great numbers, and those squires who were to be knighted watched their arms that night; they amounted to forty-six; each squire had his chamber and bath. The next day after mass the duke created them knights, and presented them with long green coats with straight sleeves lined with miniver, after the manner of the prelates. These knights had on their left shoulder a double cord of white silk, with white tufts hanging down.

This Sunday after dinner the duke left the Tower on his return to Westminster; he was bare-headed, and had round his neck the order of the King of France. The Prince of Wales, six dukes, six earls, and eighteen barons accompanied him; and of the nobility there were from 800 to 900 horse in the procession. The duke, after the German fashion, was dressed in a jacket of cloth of gold, and mounted on a white courser, with a blue garter on his left leg. He passed through the streets of London, which were at the time all handsomely decorated with tapestries and other rich hangings; there were nine fountains in Cheapside and other streets through which he passed, and these perpetually ran with white and red wine.

He was escorted by prodigious numbers of gentlemen, with their servants in livery and badges; and the different companies of London were led by their wardens, clothed in their proper livery, and with the ensigns of their trade: the whole cavalcade amounted to 6,000 horse. That same night the duke bathed, and on the morrow confessed himself, and according to his custom heard three masses.

The prelates and clergy who had been assembled then came in procession from Westminster Abbey, to conduct the king to the Tower, and back again in the same manner. The dukes, earls, and barons wore long scarlet robes, with mantles trimmed with ermine, and large hoods of the same, the dukes and earls had three bars of ermine on the left arm a quarter of a yard long, or thereabout; the barons had but two; all the knights and squires had uniform cloaks of scarlet lined with miniver. In the procession to the church the duke had borne over his head a rich canopy of blue silk, supported on silver staves, with four golden bells at the corners. This canopy was borne by four burgesses of Dover, who claimed it as their right. On each side of the duke were the sword of mercy and the sword of justice; the first being borne by the Prince of Wales, and the other by the Earl of Northumberland, Constable of England; the Earl of Westmoreland, the Marshal of England, carried the sceptre. The procession entered the church about nine o'clock. In the middle of the church was erected a scaffold covered with crimson cloth, in the centre of which was the royal throne of cloth of gold. When the duke entered the church, he seated himself on the throne, and was thus in regal state, except having the crown on his head. The Archbishop of Canterbury proclaimed from the four corners of the scaffold how God had given them a man for their lord and sovereign, and then asked the people if they were consenting parties to his being consecrated and crowned king. Upon which the people unanimously shouted 'ay', and held up their hands, promising fealty and homage.

The duke then descended from the throne and advanced to the altar to be consecrated. Two archbishops and ten bishops performed the ceremony. He was stripped of all his royal state before the altar, naked to his shirt, and was then anointed and consecrated at six places: on the head, the breast, the two shoulders, before and behind; on the back, and hands: a bonnet was then placed on his head, and while this was being done, the clergy chanted the litany, or the service that is performed to hallow a font. The king was now dressed in a churchman's clothes, like a deacon; and they put on him shoes of crimson velvet after the manner of a prelate. Then they added spurs with a point, but no rowel; and the sword of justice was drawn, blessed, and delivered to the king, who put it again into the scabbard, when the Archbishop of Canterbury [Thomas Arundel] girded it about him. The crown of St. Edward, which is arched over like a cross, was next brought, and blessed, and placed by the archbishop on the king's head. When mass was over the king left the church, and returned to the palace, in the same state as before. In the court-yard of the palace there was a fountain that ran constantly with red and white wine. The king went first to his closet, and then returned to the hall to dinner. At the first table sat the king; at the second, five great peers of England; at the third, the principal citizens of London; at the fourth the new created knights; at the fifth, all knights and squires of honour. The king was served by the Prince of Wales who carried the sword of mercy; and on the opposite side, by the constable, who bore the sword of justice. At the bottom of the table was the Earl of Westmoreland with the sceptre. At the king's table there were only the two arch-bishops and seventeen bishops.

When dinner was half over, a knight of the name of Dymock entered the hall completely armed, and mounted on a handsome steed, richly barbed with crimson housings. The knight was armed for wager of battle, and was preceded by another knight bearing his lance. He himself had his drawn sword in one hand, and his naked dagger by his side. The knight presented the king with a written paper, the contents of which were, that if any knight or gentleman should dare to maintain that King Henry was not a lawful sovereign, he was ready to offer him combat in the presence of the king, when and where he should be pleased to appoint.

The king ordered this challenge to be proclaimed by heralds, in six different parts of the town and the hall; and to it no answer was made.

King Henry having dined and partaken of wine and spices in the hall, retired to his private apartments, and all the company separated. Thus passed the coronation day of King Henry.

◆

Ordinance for the Royal Household (1279)

Source: T. F. Tout, *Medieval Administrative History* (1920–33), Vol. II pp. 158–60, trans. Stephenson/Marcham, *op. cit.*, pp. 170–2

. . . It is ordained and commanded that the stewards, or one of them if both cannot be there together, with the treasurer, or the comptroller if the treasurer cannot be there, one of the marshals of the hall, and the clerks and serjeants of the offices shall be present each night for drawing up the account of the household. And there, by witness of the ushers of the hall, the servings of food in the hall are to be checked; and according to the number of the servings, the issues from the pantry, butlery, and kitchen are to be checked. And if there is irregularity, let it be corrected and the serjeants be reproved. Each night on the margin of the household roll is to be written the amount of wine dispensed during the day; so that, by the testimony of this roll which bears the record of the household, we may two or three times a year audit the account of the tuns of wine dispensed. Next the wages of the serjeants, squires, and grooms are to be there examined, as has been accustomed. And if at the account any wrongdoing is presented which is not so bad as to require being brought to the king's attention, let it be punished there at the discretion of the stewards and the treasurer—by the witholding of wages or in some other way according to what they may think best—so that the lord king shall not be bothered with affairs that can be settled by those officials.

The treasurer, having called to him one of the stewards, or both of them, shall once or twice in every year audit the account of the chamberlain of wines; so that he may clearly know how many pieces come from each port and from each ship, and the names of the persons from whom the wines have been taken, parcel by parcel, and how much is through purchase and how much through prise. And this account is to be audited and checked by the treasurer and one of the stewards in such fashion that the treasurer can present a summary of it in his account at the feast of St. Edmund the King, when he renders his account.

In the same way the treasurer shall draw up the account of the great wardrobe. . . . And it is to be noted that the treasurer shall henceforth have all articles for the great wardrobe bought at three fairs a year by a certain man, who shall be keeper of the great wardrobe and shall go to fairs to make the purchases; and he shall be put on oath to the king for this particular office. And the usher of the wardrobe shall be comptroller for him, going to fairs with him to view his purchases and at the account witnessing liveries made by him. . . . And the aforesaid keeper shall not purchase anything or deliver anything to anybody without the special command of the treasurer, and this in the presence of the comptroller. . . .

The usher of the wardrobe should each day have the wax and candle-wicks weighed—what is to be made into candles and what is to be kept. And each night he should weigh what is given out in livery and on the morrow reweigh what is left; so that through such weights he may know what has been dispensed each night, and the sum of it all at the end of the year. . . . And the chandler shall have nothing in his charge except what is to be dispensed at night, as delivered to him by the usher.

And whereas it is rightful that the household of Madame the queen should be regulated according to the ordinance of the king's household, it is ordered that the steward of Madame, or the man who is in charge of her household, shall each night be present at the account of the king's household, together with the pantler, the butler, the chief cook, and the marshal of her chamber. . . .

Furthermore, it is ordained that the marshals, or one of them, shall make the circuit of the household each month of the year, or more often if they see fit, to clear it of rascally men and women, and of horses belonging to them, so that they shall take no hay, or oats, or wages. And the marshals shall do the same for the household of Madame. And the marshals of the hall and the ushers shall also see to it that the hall is well cleared of strange people and of rascals who should not eat there, and that the hall is served well and for the common good and that no knight has more than one squire eating in the hall.

The evening livery of wine and candles shall all be made by the king's men, as well for the household of Madame as elsewhere. And the treasurer and stewards shall see to it that no liveries are made outside except in a proper place, neither of bread nor of wine nor of candles; and each night they shall examine the liveries for the household of Madame as well as for other places and for the king's household.

Furthermore, it is ordained that no one shall sleep in the wardrobe except the treasurer; Sir Thomas Gunneys, the comptroller, Master William of Louth, the treasurer's clerk; Master Simon, the surgeon; Orlandino,[1] when he comes to court; William of Blyborough and Sire Stephen of St. George, clerks of the wardrobe; John Rede, chief usher of the wardrobe, and a footman under him —no others.

And it is ordained that no clerk who holds a benefice of the king shall henceforth receive wages from the king. And it is ordained that no one shall eat in the wardrobe except the under-usher; and the chamberlain, the treasurer, and all the other chamberlains shall eat in the hall unless they are lodged apart from the court.

With regard to the king's carriage, it is provided that for the wardrobe there shall be three long carts; for the pantry a long cart and a short one, which is to carry the demesne flour and the mills of the saucery; for the butlery a long cart and a short one; for the kitchen a long cart and two short ones.

Twenty men are chosen as serjeants-at-arms . . . and each is to receive $3\frac{1}{2}$ marks a year for robes. . . . Besides, it is ordained that each squire shall receive 10s. a year for robes, and each serving man

1. of Lucca, the king's banker.

1 mark. And each groom who received 2d. a day as wages is to have 10s. for robes; and each groom who received 1½d. a day, and all the others who ought to have robes, are to have half a mark. . . .

✧

The Knight

Source: Geoffrey Chaucer, *Canterbury Tales*, ed. N. Coghill (1951), pp. 26–7

There was a Knight, a most distinguished man,
Who from the day on which he first began
To ride abroad had followed chivalry,
Truth, honour, generous thought and courtesy.
He had done nobly in his sovereign's war
And ridden into battle, no man more,
As well in christian as in heathen places,
And ever honoured for his noble graces.
    He saw the town of Alexandria fall;
Often, at feasts, the highest place of all
Among the nations fell to him in Prussia.
In Lithuania he had fought, and Russia,
No christian man so often, of his rank,
And he was in Granada when they sank
The town of Algeciras, also in
North Africa, right through Benamarin;
And in Armenia he had been as well
And fought when Ayas and Attalia fell,
For all along the Mediterranean coast
He had embarked with many a noble host.
In fifteen mortal battles he had been
And jousted for our faith at Tramissene

Thrice in the lists, and always killed his man.
This same distinguished knight had led the van
Once with the Bey of Balat, doing work
For him against another heathen Turk;
He was of sovereign value in all eyes.
And though so much distinguished, he was wise
And in his bearing modest as a maid.
He never yet a boorish thing had said
In all his life to any, come what might;
He was a very parfit gentleknight.

Speaking of his appearance, he possessed
Fine horses, but he was not gaily dressed.
He wore a fustian tunic stained and dark
With smudges where his armour had left mark;
Just home from service, he had joined our ranks
To do his pilgrimage and render thanks.

❖

Two Squires

i. *Source: op. cit.,* pp. 27–8

He had his son with him, a fine young Squire,
A lover and cadet, a lad of fire
With curly locks, as if they had been pressed.
He was some twenty years of age, I guessed.
In stature he was of a moderate length,
With wonderful agility and strength.
He'd seen some service with the cavalry
In Flanders and Artois and Picardy
And had done valiantly in little space
Of time, in hope to win his lady's grace.
He was embroidered like a meadow bright

And full of freshest flowers, red and white.
Singing he was, or fluting all the day;
He was as fresh as is the month of May.
Short was his gown, the sleeves were long and wide;
He knew the way to sit a horse and ride.
He could make songs and poems and recite,
Knew how to joust and dance, to draw and write.
He loved so hotly that till dawn grew pale
He slept as little as a nightingale.
Courteous he was, lowly and serviceable,
And carved to serve his father at the table.

ii. *Source: Blonde of Oxford*, trans. G. G. Coulton, *Social Life in Britain from the Conquest to the Reformation* (1918), pp. 286–7

Fair, and fairer still than I can say, was Blonde the Earl's daughter. She sat at dinner, and was served by Jehan, fair and free of body, who pained himself much to earn all men's grace by his courteous service. He waited not on his lady alone, but up and down throughout the hall; knight and lady, squire and page, groom and messenger, all he served according to their desire, and thus from all he earned good-will. He knew well to seize the moment for serving and honouring each guest, so that Blonde, the fair and shapely, found her needs none the worse supplied.

After dinner they washed their hands, and went to play, each as he would, up in the forest or down by the river or in some other sort of pastime. Jehan went with whom he would; and, on his return, oftentimes would he go to play in the countess's bower, wherein the ladies, as it were by main force, kept him to teach them French. He, as a courteous youth, did and said ever according to their prayer, as one who well knew how to comport himself. Well he knew all chamber games—chess and tables and dice, wherewith he diverted the lady Blonde; often said he check and mate to her. Many other games he taught her; and taught her a better French than she had known before his coming; wherefore she held him full dear. . . .

One day, as Blonde sat at table, it was for Jehan to carve before her. . . . By chance he cast his eyes on her; yet he had seen her daily these eighteen weeks past. . . . From this look such thoughts came into his head, that on his carving he thought no more. Blonde, who marked his thoughts astray, took upon her to rebuke him therefore, and bade him think on his carving without delay. Seeing then that Jehan heard her not for the moment, then spake she again, 'Carve Jehan! are you sleeping or dreaming here? I pray you, give me now to eat; of your courtesy, dream now no more.' At this word Jehan heard her voice; therewith he started as one who is shaken suddenly from his sleep. He marvelled at this adventure; he seized the knife as a man in a dream, and thought to carve well and fair, but so distraught was he that he cut deep into two fingers: forth sprang the blood as he rose from the table, and sad was Blonde at that sight. Jehan prayed another squire to carve before his lady, and went forthwith to his own chamber.

❧

The Yeoman

Source: Geoffrey Chaucer, *Canterbury Tales*, ed. N. Coghill, p. 28

> There was a Yeoman with him at his side,
> No other servant, so he chose to ride.
> This Yeoman wore a coat and hood of green,
> And peacock-feathered arrows, bright and keen
> And neatly sheathed, hung at his belt the while,
> —For he could dress his gear in yeoman style,
> His arrows never drooped their feathers low—
> And in his hand he bore a mighty bow.
> His head was like a nut, his face was brown.
> He knew the whole of woodcraft up and down.

A saucy brace was on his arm to ward
It from the bow-string, and a shield and sword
Hung at one side, and at the other slipped
A jaunty dirk, spear-sharp and well-equipped.
A medal of St. Christopher he wore
Of shining silver on his breast, and bore
A hunting-horn, well slung and burnished clean
That dangled from a baldrick of bright green.
He was a proper forester I guess.

❖

Games Supplant Archery (1363)

Source: Rymer, *Foedera*, Vol. III, *Readings in English Social History*, ed. R. B. Morgan (1923), pp. 150–1

The King [Edward III] to the Lord-lieutenant of Kent, greeting: Whereas the people of our realm, rich and poor alike, were accustomed formerly in their games to practise archery—whence by God's help, it is well known that high honour and profit came to our realm, and no small advantage to ourselves in our warlike enterprises—and that now skill in the use of the bow having fallen almost wholly into disrepute, our subjects give themselves up to the throwing of stones and of wood and of iron; and some to handball and football and hockey; and others to coursing and cockfights, and even to other unseemly sports less useful and manly; whereby our realm—which God forbid—will soon, it would appear, be void of archers:

We, wishing that a fitting remedy be found in this matter, do hereby ordain, that in all places in your county, liberties or no liberties, wheresoever you shall deem fit, a proclamation be made to this effect: that every man in the same county, if he be able-bodied,

shall upon holidays, make use, in his games, of bows and arrows
. . . and so learn and practise archery.

Moreover we ordain that you prohibit under penalty of imprisonment all and sundry from such stone, wood and iron throwing;
handball, football, or hockey; coursing and cock-fighting; or other
such idle games.

✦

Froissart's Youth

Source: trans. G. G. Coulton, *op. cit.,* pp. 84–5

In my youth, such was my temper that I loved pastime passing
well; and, as I was then, such am I still, though yesterday be not
today. While I was yet but twelve years old, I hungered and
thirsted to see dances and carols, to hear minstrels and words of
solace; so it was my nature to love hotly all such as love hawks and
hounds. When therefore I was put to school, wherein the ignorant
are taught, I found there the little girls whose tender youth was
even as mine own; and I, who was a little boy, would serve them
with gifts of pins or apples or pears, or with a ring of glass; and, for
to say sooth, methought it was great prowess to win their grace—
as in truth it is; for I say none otherwise to-day. And then I was wont
to think in my heart 'When will my day come, that I shall be able
to love in very sooth?' for thereunto was my nature inclined, and
everywhere men proclaim that all joy and all honour cometh from
arms and from love. . . . But what age, to say truth, think ye that I
had when Love, by his wounds, taught me his precious balms?
Very young I was in years: never yet had I tired of children's games
as they are played before the age of twelve. When I was grown a
little wise, then I must needs to be more fully subject to my masters;
for they taught me the Latin tongue, and, if I varied in repeating my
lessons, I was beaten. . . . I could not rest; for I fought with other

children, beat and was beaten; so distraught was I that I oftentimes
went home with torn raiment; there again I was reproached full oft
or beaten. But be assured that my parents lost their labour; for this
never turned me aside, but, as soon as I saw my fellows pass by on
their way, full soon I found some excuse to escape and join their
play.

But, so help me God! so happily did I pass those days that all
things turned unto me for delight, whether speech or silence,
whether movement or rest, for I had time at my choice. In those
days I took more account of a chaplet of violets to give to those
little girls, than I take now for twenty silver marks from the hand
of a count. . . . Though my body was yet weak and tender, yet my
heart would fain be everywhere, and specially wheresoever there
was plenty of violets and roses and peonies, wherein (God help me!)
I took more delight than in aught else. And when the season
changed and winter came, with his rain and foul weather, then I
delighted to take my pastime in reading romances, and specially
such as treated of love.

✦

Courting in the Fifteenth Century

Source: The Cely Letters, quoted J. J. Bagley, *Historical Interpretation*
(1965), pp. 181–2

The same day that I come to Northleach on a Sunday before
mattins from Burford William Midwinter welcomed me and in our
communication he asked me if I were in any way of marriage. I
told him nay, and he informed me that there was a young gentlewoman whose father's name is Lemryke and her mother is dead and
she shall inherit from her mother £40 a year as they say in that
country, and her father is the greatest ruler as richest man in that

country. . . . When I had packed [the wool] at Camden and William Midwinter departed I came to Northleach again to make an end of packing, and on Sunday next after, the same man that William Midwinter brake first came to me and told me that he had broken to his master according as Midwinter desired him . . . and if I would tarry till May Day I should have a sight of the young gentlewoman, and I said I would tarry with a good will . . . to mattins the same day come the young gentlewoman and her mother-in-law, and I and William Bretten were saying mattins when they come into church, and when mattins were done they went to a kinswoman of the young gentlewoman and I sent to them a pottle of white romnay and they took it thankfully for they had come a mile afoot that morning and when mass was done I come and welcomed them and kissed them and they thanked me for the wine and prayed me to come to dinner with them, and I excused me and they made me promise to drink with them after dinner, and I sent them to dinner a gallon of wine and they sent me a roast heron, and after dinner I come and drank with them and took William Bretten with me and we had right good communication, and the person pleased me well, as by the first communication she is young, little and very well-favoured and witty and the country speaks much good by her. Sir, all this matter abideth the coming of her father to London that we may understand what sum he will depart with and how he likes me. He will be here within three weeks. I pray send me a letter how you think by this manner. . . . Writ at London the 13 day of May per Richard Cely.

Fourteenth Century Fashion

i. *Source:* Thomas Hoccleve, *The Regiment of Princes*, quoted J. J. Bagley, *Historical Interpretation* (1965), p. 138

> But this me thinketh an abusion,
> To see one walk in gowns of scarlet,
> Twelve yards wide, with pendant sleeves down
> On the ground, and the rich fur therein set.
> Amounting to twenty pound or better;
> And if he for it have paid, he no good
> Hath left him wherewith for to buy a hood.

ii. Geoffrey Chaucer, *The Canterbury Tales*, ed. N. Coghill (1951), pp. 114–15

> There was a parish clerk
> Serving the church whose name was Absolon.
> His hair was all in golden curls and shone,
> Just like a fan it strutted outwards, starting
> To left and right from an accomplished parting.
> Ruddy his face, his eyes as grey as goose,
> His shoes cut out in tracery, as in use
> In old St. Pauls. The hose upon his feet
> Showed scarlet through, and all his clothes were neat
> And proper. In a jacket of light blue,
> Flounced at the waist and tagged with laces too,
> He went, and wore a surplice just as gay
> And white as any blossom of the spray.
> God bless my soul, he was a merry knave!
> He knew how to let blood, cut hair and shave,
> And draw up legal deeds; at other whiles
> He used to dance in twenty different styles
> (After the current school at Oxford though,

Casting his legs about him to and fro).
He played a two-stringed fiddle, did it proud,
And sang a high falsetto rather loud;
And he was just as good on the guitar.
There was no public-house in town or bar
He didn't visit with his merry face
If there were saucy barmaids round the place.

✦

The Wife of Bath

Source: op. cit., pp. 37–8

A worthy woman from beside Bath city
Was with us, somewhat deaf, which was a pity.
In making cloth she showed so great a bent
She bettered those of Ypres and of Ghent.
In all the parish not a dame dared stir
Towards the altar steps in front of her,
And if indeed they did, so wrath was she
As to be quite put out of charity.
Her kerchiefs were of finely woven ground;
I dared have sworn they weighed a good ten pound,
The ones she wore on Sunday, on her head.
Her hose were of the finest scarlet red
And gartered tight; her shoes were soft and new.
Bold was her face, handsome, and red in hue.
A worthy woman all her life, what's more
She'd had five husbands, all at the church door,
Apart from other company in youth;
No need just now to speak of that, forsooth.
And she had thrice been to Jerusalem,

Seen many strange rivers and passed over them;
She'd been to Rome and also to Boulogne,
St. James of Compostella and Cologne,
And she was skilled in wandering by the way.
She had gap-teeth, set widely, truth to say.
Easily on an ambling horse she sat
All wimpled up, and on her head a hat
As broad as is a buckler or a shield;
She had a flowing mantle that concealed
Large hips, her heels spurred sharply under that.
In company she liked to laugh and chat
And knew the remedies for love's mischances,
An art in which she knew the oldest dances.

The Birth of a Chronicle

Source: The Annals of Ghent, ed. H. Johnstone (1951), p. 1

One day when I was not very busy, it occurred to me that as I enjoy reading and hearing stories and true facts about old times, and write quickly, and also had at my disposal a stock of small membranes of no great value, stitched together, I might set forth on them, in chronological order, in an easy, light, and clear style, those manifold battles and perils, distresses and oppressions of various kinds, expeditions, sieges, and attacks both passive and active, which had befallen our land of Flanders, and the divers happenings of my times—at all of which I was either present and an eye-witness, or else ascertained the facts with certainty from the relation of those who were present—and leave it to posterity, if interested in reading and hearing such things, to register them in a subtler and finer fashion. Now I started this, about the beginning of the year of our

Lord 1308, in the house of the Friars Minor at Ghent, of which I was then a member. My motive was to please and entertain some of the brothers who at times enjoyed hearing or reading such things. Moreover, I had in mind the common welfare, for, so it seems to me, when any events are sinking into oblivion it is most useful to know about them. Note that the years of our Lord which follow are always to be begun on the feast of the Annunciation of the Blessed Virgin, that is to say, on March 25, however the feast of Easter may vary.

✦

Two Monastic Historians

I. MATTHEW PARIS

Source: Thomas Walsingham, *Deeds of the Abbots*, ed. H. T. Riley (1867–9), Vol. I p. 395, trans. G. G. Coulton, *op. cit.*, p. 126

In his time [Abbot John II, 1235–60] flourished and died Dom Matthew Paris, monk of St. Albans, a man of eloquence and renown, fulfilled of innumerable virtues, a magnificent historiographer and chronographer, a most excellent composer in the Latin tongue, and one who kept that saying in his heart: 'idleness is the enemy of the soul'. This man's fame was so spread abroad that it had recommended him even to men of remote parts who had never seen his face. He collected from ancient times even unto the end of his own life, and wrote down fully in his books, the deeds of great men in Church and State, with sundry and marvellous chances and events, whereby he bequeathed to posterity a marvellous knowledge of the past. Moreover he was so subtle a workman in gold and silver and other metals, in carving and in painting, that he is believed to have left no equal in this world of the West. Let us therefore take him for

our pattern, and labour without ceasing at wholesome works, that
we may share with him in the rewards of heaven.

2. THOMAS BURTON

Source: Chronicle of Meaux, ed. E. H. Bond (1866–8), Vol. I p. 71,
trans. G. G. Coulton, *op. cit.*, pp. 146–7

When I see how the memory of the famous men who have been
abbots of this house of Meaux hath almost utterly perished through
the sloth of negligent men, I am grieved to the heart and must
grievously groan and sigh; not only because so many and excellent
lights of the church (that is, so many glorious deeds of our noble
ancestors) are hidden and set under a bushel, but also because so
many wise and learned men our predecessors, while they feared not
to heap up the treasures of their own wisdom, took no heed to
commit to public writing the praiseworthy acts of their forefathers.
I therefore, desiring to put an end to this great negligence so far as
in me lay (though I knew well mine own utter unworthiness for the
task), have at length, after tedious scrutiny, collected together certain ancient scrolls and neglected parchments, some of which I
found exposed to the rain [that dripped through the roof], and
others set aside to be burned. In these documents I have abridged
whatsoever was too lengthy, and explained more clearly whatsoever was obscure; I have perused the registers, and filled in their
omissions from other registers or trustworthy documents; and
these collections I have at last compiled into the following work.
Therefore, if any reader find herein matters whereof he knew
nothing, let him not suppose that I have composed them out of
mine own head; let him rather be assured that there is nothing in
this book but such as I have either found written in other men's
books, or from divers written records, or from frequent and trustworthy hearsay, or from that which I myself have seen. Accordingly
I beseech all who shall read this chronicle, such as it is, either to
blush that they themselves do nothing to correct ancient neglect,
or at least to be ashamed of carping at me who am attempting to

amend [this neglect]. Moreover, if any be offended at my brevity of narration or at the rudeness of my style, there will be nothing to hinder any other from writing another such book after his own fashion; nay, he may do so the more easily, in proportion as the truth is more clearly narrated in this work.

✦

Advice to Oxford Undergraduates (1293)

Source: Simon of Ghent, Chancellor of Oxford, Sermon on Ash Wednesday, 1293, *Oxford Theology and Theologians*, A. G. Little and F. Pelster (1932), pp. 205–6, quoted *The English Church in the Fourteenth Century*, W. A. Pantin (1962), p. 112

For the serpent said: 'Why are you forbidden to eat of every tree of paradise?' And Eve answered: 'Lest by chance we die.' But the serpent said: 'By no means, but you shall be like gods.' Is not that just the way some go on nowadays, seducing others? 'Why are you forbidden to go into taverns, to play after curfew, to go into the houses of lay folk?' One will reply: 'Lest by chance I am excommunicated or imprisoned or some such evil befall me.' 'By no means,' says another, 'let us go and play; don't let us give it up for such reasons.' And so they draw many after them and deceive them. I have heard this year about some who have in this way persuaded others to play and led them into thieving, have gone to the tavern and then drawn them to the brothel, have persuaded them to a trial of strength and have ended up with manslaughter. I have even found this to be true, that some have led their friends to the tavern, and when they have got there, others have tried to cut their throats. . . . For who are more obstinate nowadays than clerks? Who is there among the laity that is not kept from evil by the fear of punishment

195

or loss? Who that does not fear the sentence of excommunication? But clerks fear neither the temporal nor spiritual penalty nor excommunication. . . . Remember, O clerk, chosen to God's lot. Your friends perhaps have worked hard to maintain you in the schools, that you may profit yourself and others. Now you are neither profiting yourself nor others, nay you are only hurting them and wasting your parents' money in evil uses. Those who used to have hope of your promotion have now given you up in despair.

The Oxford Scholar

Source: Geoffrey Chaucer, *Canterbury Tales,* ed. N. Coghill, p. 33

There was an Oxford Cleric too, a student,
Long given to Logic, longer than was prudent;
The horse he had was leaner than a rake,
And he was not too fat, I undertake,
But had a hollow look, a sober stare;
The thread upon his overcoat was bare.
He had found no preferment in the church
And he was too unworldly to make search.
He thought far more of having by his bed
His twenty books all bound in black and red,
Of Aristotle and philosophy
Than of gay music, fiddles or finery.
Though a philosopher, as I have told,
He had not found the stone for making gold.
Whatever money from his friends he took
He spent on learning or another book
And prayed for them most earnestly, returning
Thanks to them thus for paying for his learning.

His only care was study, and indeed
He never spoke a word more than was need,
Formal at that, respectful in the extreme,
Short, to the point, and lofty in his theme.
The thought of moral virtue filled his speech
And he would gladly learn, and gladly teach.

✦

Fifteenth Century Regulations at King's College, Cambridge

Source: King's College and Eton College Statutes, ed. J. Heywood and T. Wright (1850), trans. G. G. Coulton *op. cit.*, pp. 72–3

We ordain that our students go not about alone, without a fellow or scholar of the said King's College, or one of the common servants thereof, or some other companion of mature age and good character; and let them walk modestly and without confusion—save only to processions, sermons, churches, or the Schools, for which purposes we permit them to go alone if they cannot well find such a companion. Further, we prohibit all and singular the fellows and scholars aforesaid from wearing red or green hosen, piked shoes, or striped hoods, on any pretext, within or without the University or the town of Cambridge, either publicly or privately, except for some necessary cause to be approved by the Provost, or by the Vice-Provost, Deans, and Bursars. Furthermore we ordain that no scholar or fellow let his hair or beard grow; but that all wear the crown and tonsure,[1] accordant to their order, degree, and condition, honestly and duly and decently.

1. By the *corona* the hair was cropped close to the ears and the nape of the neck; by the *tonsura* a small bald patch was made at the top; but *tonsura* is often used for both operations.

Since it befitteth not poor men, and specially such as live by charity, to give the children's bread unto dogs . . . therefore we command, ordain and will that no scholar, fellow, chaplain, clerk, or servant whatsoever to the said King's College, do keep or possess dogs, hunting or fishing nets, ferrets, falcons, or hawks; nor shall they practise hunting or fishing. Nor shall they in any wise have or hold within our Royal College, singly or in common, any ape, bear, fox, stag, hind, fawn, or badger, or any other such ravening or unaccustomed or strange beast, which are neither profitable nor unprofitable. Furthermore, we forbid and expressly interdict the games of dice, hazard, ball and all noxious inordinate unlawful and unhonest sports, and especially all games which afford a cause or occasion for loss of coin, money, goods or chattels of any kind whatsoever, whether within King's College or elsewhere within the University. . . . And it is Our will firmly and expressly to prohibit all of the aforesaid fellows &c. from shooting arrows, or casting or hurling stones, javelins, wood, clods or anything whatsoever, and from making or practising, singly or in common, in person or by deputy, any games or castings whatsoever, within the aforesaid King's College or its enclosed precincts or gardens, whereby, directly or indirectly, the Chapel or Hall or other buildings or edifices of our said College may suffer any sort of harm or loss in the glass windows, walls, roofs, coverings, or any other part thereof within or without. Item: whereas through incautious and inordinate games in the Chapel or Hall of our said King's College, which might perchance be practised therein by the wantonness of some students, the said Chapel and Hall might be harmed and even deformed in its walls, stalls, paintings and glass windows; we therefore, desiring to provide against such harm, do strictly command that no casting of stones or balls or of anything else soever be made in the aforesaid collegiate Chapel, Cloister, Stalls, or Hall; and we forbid that dancing or wrestling, or other incautious and inordinate sports whatsoever, be practised at any time within the Chapel, Cloister or Hall aforesaid.

❖

Chaucer and His Books

i. *Source: House of Fame*, ed. W. W. Skeat (1897), lines 652–9

> For when thy labour done all is,
> And hast made all thy reckonings,
> Instead of rest and new things,
> Thou goest home to thy house anon;
> And, as dumb as any stone,
> Thou sittest at another book
> Till fully dazed in thy look,
> And livest thus as an hermit,
> Although thine abstinence is light.

ii. *Source: Legend of Good Women*, ed. W. W. Skeat (1897), lines 25–37

> And if that old books were away,
> Lost were of remembrance the key
> Well ought us then to honour and believe
> These books, there we have none other proof.
> And as for me, though that I can but light
> On books for to read I me delight,
> And to them give I faith and full credence,
> And in mine heart have them in reverence
> So heartily, that there is game none
> That from my books maketh me to go,
> But it be seldom on the holiday,
> Save certainly when that the month of May
> Is come. . . .

The Treatment of Books

Source: Philobiblon, Richard de Bury, trans. G. G. Coulton, *op. cit.,* pp. 185–6

You will see perchance some headstrong youth, sitting slothfully at his studies . . . his finger-nails are filthy, black as jet, and with them he marks the place where the matter takes his fancy. He distributes innumerable straws, laying them conspicuously in divers places of the book, that the wheatstalk may recall whatsoever his memory may let slip. These straws, which are never withdrawn, remain undigested in the book's belly, first distending it to the bursting of its wonted clasps, and then rotting in the neglect and oblivion to which they have been left. He shrinketh not from eating fruit or cheese over his open book, nor from moving his cup carelessly over it; and, having no bag at hand, he leaves in his book the fragments that remain. . . . Then he leans his elbows on the book and takes a long sleep in exchange for his brief study, and bends back the margins of the leaves to smooth out the wrinkles, to the no small detriment of the volume. Now the rain is over and gone, and the flowers appear on our earth; and this scholar whom we describe, this neglector rather than inspector of books, will stuff his volume with violets, primroses, roses and four-leaved clover. Then he will paw it over with hands wet with water or sweat; then with dusty gloves he will fumble over the white parchment, and hunt for his page, line by line, with a forefinger clad in this ancient leather. Then, at the prick of some biting flea, the sacred volume is cast aside, scarce to be closed again for another month, when it is so clogged and swollen with dust that it resists all efforts to close it.

But we must specially keep from all touch of our books those shameless youths who, when they have learned to shape the letters of the alphabet, straightway become incongruous annotators of all the fairest volumes that come in their way, and either deck with their monstrous alphabets all broader margins that they can find around the text, or rashly presume to write with unchastened pen whatsoever frivolous stuff may happen to run at that moment in their heads. . . . There are thieves also, who shamefully mutilate our books, cutting down the lateral margins, to the very quick of the written text, as material for their own epistolary correspondence, or stealing for various evil uses the blank pages which guard the book's ends; a sort of sacrilege which doth merit to be prohibited under strictest threat of excommunication.

Moreover, scholastic decency imperatively demands that, whensoever we return to study from our meals, we should wash our hands before reading; no finger dipped in grease should either turn the leaves or even open the clasps, before such ablution. Let no whimpering child be suffered to admire the pictures capital letters, lest his slimy hand defile the parchment; for whatsoever the child seeth, that must he also touch. The unlearned also, for whom a book is the same whether it be held open upright or topsy-turvy, are utterly unworthy of any communion with books. Let the clerk see to it also, that the sooty scullion reeking straight from the fleshpots lay no unwashen finger on the lily-white page; let him who ministereth to your precious volumes be one who walketh without blemish. A decent cleanliness of hand would be most profitable both to books and to scholars, if scabs and pustules were not marks of the clerical character.

❖

Roger Bacon's Forecasts

Source: Roger Bacon, *Epistola de Secretis*, ed. J. S. Brewer (1859), ch. 2, trans. G. G. Coulton, *op. cit.*, pp. 524–5

I will now proceed, therefore, to relate the works of art and miracles of nature, that I may afterwards expound the cause and manner thereof; wherein there is nothing magical; nay rather, all magical power would seem inferior to such works, and unworthy of them. And first I will discourse through the figure and reason of art alone. For vessels might be made to move without oars or rowers, so that ships of great size might move on sea or on river, at the governance of a single man, more swiftly than if they were strongly manned. Moreover, chariots might be made to move without animal impulse at an incalculable speed; such as we suppose those scythed chariots to have been wherewith men were wont to fight in ancient days. Again, flying instruments might be made, so that a man might sit in the midst thereof, turning a certain machine whereby wings of artful composition should beat the air, after the fashion of a bird in her flight. Another instrument might be made, of small size, to raise or lower weights of almost infinite greatness; than which nothing could be more useful in certain cases. For, by means of an instrument of the height and breadth of three fingers, and less bulk than they, a man might free himself and his companions from all peril of prison, lifting them and lowering them again. Moreover, an instrument might easily be made whereby one man could violently draw a thousand men to himself against their will, and so also of the attraction of other things. Again, instruments might be made for walking in the sea, or in rivers, even to the very bottom, without bodily danger: for Alexander the Great used these to see the secrets of the sea, as is related by Ethicus the Astronomer. For these things were done of old, and have certainly also been done in our own times; except possibly the flying machine, which I have never seen, nor have I met any man who hath seen it; but I know a wise man who hath excogitated this artifice. And almost innumerable things of this kind might be made; bridges over rivers without pier or prop whatsoever, and unheard of machines and engines.

❖

Actors

Source: Thomas of Cobham, *Penitential,* trans. G. G. Coulton, *op. cit.,* pp. 403-4

There are three kinds of play actors [*histrionum*]. Some transform and transfigure their own bodies by base contortions and base gestures, or by basely denuding themselves, or by wearing horrible masks; and all such are to be damned unless they abandon their calling. Others, again do no work, but commit criminal deeds, having no fixed abode, but haunting the courts of great men and backbiting the absent opprobriously and ignominiously in order to please others. Such men also are to be damned; for the Apostle bids us take no food with such men as this; and such men are called wandering buffoons, for they are good for nothing but gluttony and backbiting. There is also a third kind of actors who have musical instruments for men's delight; and such are of two kinds. Some haunt public drinkings and wanton assemblies, where they sing divers songs to move men to wantonness; and such are to be damned like the rest. But there are others called jongleurs [*joculatores*], who sing the deeds of princes and the lives of the saints, and solace men in their sickness or in their anguish, and do not those innumerable base deeds which are done by dancing-men and dancing-women and others who play in indecent figures, and make men see a certain show of phantasms by enchantment or in any other way. If, then, these do no such thing, but sing to their instruments of the deeds of princes and other such profitable things, for the solace of their fellow-Christians, as is aforesaid, then such may well be borne with, as was said by pope Alexander III. For, when a jongleur asked of him whether he could save his soul in that calling, the Pope asked him whether he knew any other work for his livelihood; and he made answer that he knew none. Then the Pope permitted him to live by that calling, so long as he abstained from the aforesaid base and wanton practices. And it must be noted that all commit mortal sin who give any of their goods to buffoons or jesters or the aforesaid play-actors; for to give to play-actors is no other than to throw our money away.

✦

The Beginnings of the Secular Stage

Source: John de Grandisson, *Register,* ed. H. Randolph (1897), Vol. II p. 1053, trans. G. G. Coulton, *op. cit.,* pp. 493–5

We have heard, not without grave disquietude, that a certain abominable sect of evil-minded men, named the Order (let us rather say the Error) of Brothelyngham, hath lately arisen by inspiration of him who soweth all evil deeds. Which men, forming no true covenant but rather a plainly unlawful and sinister conventicle, have chosen for their head a certain crazy lunatic, of temper most suitable to their evil purpose. This man they call their Abbot; they dress him in monastic garb, set him up upon a stage, and adore him as their idol. Then, at the sound of a horn, which they have chosen instead of a bell, they led him not many days since through the lanes and streets of the said city of Exeter, with a great throng of horse and foot at their heels; in which procession they laid hold on clergy or laity whom they found in their way—nay, they even drew some from their own houses—and held them so long in durance, with rash, headlong, and sometimes with sacrilegious spirit, until they had extorted from them certain sums of money by way of sacrifice —nay, rather, of sacrilege. And, though they seem to do this under colour and cloak of play, or rather of buffoonery, yet this is beyond doubt no other than theft and rapine, since the money is taken from the unwilling.

The envious enemy of mankind and instigator of all evil, who doth assiduously strive to banish from the world all delights of human tranquillity, is busy to spread the poison of his iniquity more widely in those places where he seeth most hope of mischief.

Although the mechanical arts, as experience ever shows us, should of necessity help one another, yet we have heard some time since that certain imprudent sons of our City of Exeter, given over to rioting and wantonness, and foolishly scorning that which had been profitably ordered for their own needs and those of the whole people, do purpose, and have banded themselves together, publicly to perform a certain noxious and blameworthy play, or rather buffoonery, in scorn and insult to the leather-dressers and their art, on this Sunday next to come and in the theatre of our aforesaid City of Exeter. Hence (as we are informed) there doth already breed and increase a rank growth of discord, rancour and strife between the aforesaid artisans and the authors or abettors of this same play; so that (unless, led by a spirit of saner counsel, they shalt altogether abstain and desist from their unlawful purpose), there must follow, alas! terrible assaults and aggressions, breaches of the peace of the king and his realm, blows and seditions, and even, by consequence, perils still more deplorable for men's immortal souls. . . .

❖

Plays and Wrestlings

Sources: i. P.R.O. Ancient Petition 4858
ii. Cartulary of St Mary, Clerkenwell, British Museum, trans. R. B. Morgan (1923), Readings in English Social History, pp. 120–1

i. To our Lord the King. The poor Prioress of Clerkenwell prays that he will to provide and order a remedy because the people of London lay waste and destroy her corn and grass by their miracle plays and wrestling matches, so that she has no profit of them nor can have unless the king have pity for they are a savage folk and we cannot stand against them and cannot get justice by any law. So, Sire, for God's sake have pity on us.

ii. Edward by the grace of God King of England Lord of Ireland and Duke of Aquitaine to the Mayor and sheriffs of London greeting. Whereas we have learnt by the earnest complaint of the Prioress of Clerkenwell, our beloved in Christ, that men of the said city on horse and on foot in great number come to the fields, meadows and pastures of the said prioress at Clerkenwell with their followers and make wrestlings and other plays there; and flatten the enclosures, hedges and ditches that are around the corn, the meadows and the pastures of the said prioress; and crush and trample the corn and grass in many ways and this is to the great loss of the said prioress and a grievance; We therefore wish to attend to the redress of the said prioress in this matter and do order you with a firm injunction that if it is thus in the said city you do have ordered and proclaimed publicly on our behalf that they do not dare in future exercise such wrestlings and plays in the fields, meadows and pastures of the said prioress whereby she can receive hurt and loss. In this we hold you that no repeated complaint reach us whereby we have to attend to this matter further. Witnessed by me at Fakenham, 8 April in the twenty-ninth year of our reign [1301].

❧

Revels

Source: The Dancers of Colbeck, quoted J. J. Bagley, *Historical Interpretation* (1965), pp. 132–3

> Carols, wrestlings, or summer games,
> Whosoever haunteth any such shames
> In church, or in churchyard,
> Of sacrilege he may be afeared;

> Or interludes, or singing,
>> Or tabor beat, or other piping—
> All such thing forbidden is
>> While the priest standeth at mass. . . .

❖

A Fourteenth Century Housewarming

Source: Annals of Ghent, ed. H. Johnstone (1951), pp. 87–8

That same month some five hundred hired entertainers, mostly youngsters of both sexes, were invited to dance at the inauguration of a new courtyard at a new house. They leapt about so much in their dancing both above, in the two solars, and below, in the courtyard, that the brick wall of the house and consequently its roof collapsed and fell. About fifty of them present were crushed and killed instantly. The rest, in complete panic, escaped death, though a hundred were seriously wounded or suffered grave internal injury.

❖

Proof of Age (1307)

Source: Calendar of Inquisitions Post Mortem (c. 1908), Vol. V, No. 67

Richard Golene of Conyton, aged 60, says the said John is 23 and more, and was born at Conyton on the day of St. Clement the Pope, 13 Edw. 1, and baptized in the church there on the morrow, which he knows because he has a son Robert of the same age, who was baptized at the same church on the same day.

John Kaym of the same, aged 50, says the same, and knows it because he is godfather of the said John, and gave him ½ mark and a gold ring.

William Quyntyn of the same, aged 54, says the same, and knows it because he married his wife Thephania in 12 Edw. 1, and buried her on the same eve of St. Clement, 13 Edw. 1, in the cemetery of Conyton, and was almost mad with grief.

Roger de Hiltone, aged 60, says the same, and recollects it because on the same day of St. Clement he held a feast in honour of the Saint, when, all his neighbours sitting at dinner, his oven and kitchen were burned.

John Pollard of Fendrayton, aged 40, says the same, which he recollects because on that day of St. Clement he was robbed and wounded almost to death by robbers.

William Jek of the same, aged 45, says the same, and knows it because on the day the said John was baptized he buried his father James in the cemetery of Conyton.

Wymund de la Grove of Elesworth, aged 58, says the same, and recollects it because in the same church and on the same day that the said John was baptized he caused to be read before the parishioners of Conyton his charters of a parcel of land which he bought there, took seisin the same day, and was ejected on the morrow.

Robert de la Brok of Elesworth, William Fraunkeleyn of Bokesworth, William Morel of Fendrayton, and John Pount and William de la Grove of Suavesheye, each 50 and more, agree, pretending their knowledge of the lapse of so much time because on the day the said John was baptized in the same church, they caused their staves and purses to be consecrated, and all together took their journey for St. Andrews in Scotland.

❖

Animals

Source: John of Trevisa, *Bartholomew the Englishman* (1398), Bk. XVIII ch. 76, 25–8, 89, quoted G. G. Coulton, *op. cit.*, pp. 371–3

The catte is a beaste of uncerten heare and colour; for some catte is white, some rede, some blacke, some skewed[1] and speckled in the fete and in the face and in the eares. . . . And he is a ful lecherous beste in youth, swyfte, plyaunte, and mery, and lepeth and reseth[2] on all thynge that is to-fore him; and is led by a strawe and playeth therwith. And is a right hevy best in aege, and ful slepy, and lyeth slily in wait for myce; and is waare where they ben more by smelle than by sight; and hunteth and reseth on them in prevye places; and when he taketh a mous he playeth therwith, and eateth him after the play. And is as it were wilde, and gothe about among cattes. In tyme of love is harde fighting for wives, and one cratchethe and rentethe the other grevously with bytyng and with clawes. And he maketh a ruthefull noyse and gastfull, whan one proffreth to fyghte with another . . . and falleth on his owne fete whan he fallth out of hye places.

Nothing is more besy and wittyer than an hound, for he hath more wit than other bestis. And houndes knowe theyr owne names, and love their maisters, and defend the houses of their maisters, and put themselfe wilfullye in peryll of deth for their maisters, and ren to take proies for their maisters and forsake not the deed bodyes of theyr maysters. And houndes pursue the fote of proie by smel of blood, and love company of men, and maye nat be withoute men. . . . Amonge beastes that dwell with us, houndes and horses ben mooste gracious. We have knowen that houndes faught for theyr lordes agaynst theves and were sore wounded, and that they kept away beastes and foules fro theyr maysters bodyes deed. And that an hounde compelled the sleer of his master with berkynge and

1. piebald.
2. rusheth.

bytynge to knowledge his trespas and gylte. . . . The cruelness of an hound abateth to a meke man.

Houndes have other proprites that ben not ful good, for houndes have contynualle Bolisme, that is immoderate appetyte. . . . Also an hounde is wrathefull and malycyous, soo that, for to awreke hym selfe, he byteth ofte the stoon that is throwen to hym, and byteth the ston with gret wodnesse[1] that he breketh his owne teethe and greveth not the stone, but his owne teethe full sore. Also he is gylefull and dysceyvable, and so ofte he fyckelythe[2] and fawneth with his taylle on menne that passethe by the waye, as though he weere a frende; and byteth them sore, (yf they take none hede) backwarde. . . . Also he is covetous and glotonous . . . and he gadryth herbes prively, by whom he purgeth hymselfe, and hathe envye and is ryghte sorye if any man knowith the vertu of those herbes. And is also evyll-apayd[3] if any straunge houndes and un-knowen come in to the place there he dwellethe, and dredeth lest he shulde fare the worse for the other houndes presence, and fyghteth with hym therfore. Also he is covetous and scarse[4] and besy to laye up and to hyde the releyf[5] that he leveth. And therfore he comyneth[6] not ne yeveth fleshe and mariboones, that he may not devour, to other houndes, but layeth them uppe besyly and hydeth them until he hungreth ayen . . . Aristotle sayth, that houndes in age have the podagre,[7] and fewe of them scape that evil, and there-fore they slepe in daye time. . . . And though [the flies] bite and perce somtyme the houndes eares, yet for slouth he taketh no comforte and strength to chace and dryve them awaye, but unneth[8] whan they flye ayenst his face he snatcheth at them with his mouthe, and besiethe to bite them with his teethe. And at the laste the scabbed hounde is vyolently drawen out of the dounghyl with a rope or with a whyp bounde abowt his necke, and is drowned in the ryver, or in some other water, and so he endeth his wretched lyfe. And his skynne is not taken of, nor his fleshe is not eate nor buryed, but left finally to flyes and to other dyvers wormes. . . . Houndes that ben ordeyned to kepyng of houses sholde be closed and bounde in a derke place by daye, and soo they benne the

1. madness. 2. flattereth. 3. ill-pleased. 4. miserly.
5. remnants. 6. shareth. 7. gout. 8. scarcely.

stronger by nyght, and the more cruell ayenste theves.

The flee is a lyttell worme, and greveth men mooste; and scapeth and voideth peril with lepynge and not with rennynge, and wexeth slowe and fayleth in colde tyme, and in somer tyme it wexeth quiver[1] and swyft; and spareth not kynges.

✦

The Ghost of the Gog Magog Hills

Source: Gervase of Tilbury, ed. F. Liebrecht (1856), ch. LIX p. 26, trans. G. G. Coulton, *op. cit.,* pp. 532–4

In England, on the confines of the diocese of Ely, is a town named Cambridge, within whose bounds, and hard by the town, lieth a place which men call Wandlebury, for that the Vandals had their camp there when they invaded Britain and cruelly slaughtered the Christians. On the spot where they pitched their tents, at the very summit of the hill, is a level space girt and ringed round by earthen banks, with but one opening for ingress, after the fashion of a gate. The aforesaid level field hath this property from time immemorial (and common report beareth witness thereunto) that if, after nightfall, any knight enter therein and cry aloud: 'Let a knight come against this knight!' forthwith a knight will rush forward to meet him, full armed for the fray; then will the two horsemen fall upon each other; and one or other will be overthrown. Yet it must be premised, by way of warning, that the knight must enter this enclosure alone, though his companions may be suffered to wait and gaze without. In witness of this matter I add an event which is known to many, far and near, and which I have myself heard from those who were born and have dwelt near to this spot. There was in Britain, not long since, a most doughty knight,

1. alert.

endowed with every virtue, surpassed in power by few among the barons, and in probity by none; his name was Osbert Fitz-Hugh. One day this knight entered the town of Cambridge as a guest; and, after support, his host's family sat by the fire to tell and listen of ancient deeds as great men are wont to do; for his host was a man of wealth. At length one of the Cambridge men related the story of Wandlebury; whereat this doughty knight resolved to prove by experience the tale which he had heard with his ears. Choosing one of his noble squires, he went with him to the hill, and found the camp. Here, clad in full armour, he mounted his horse and drew near; and, leaving his squire without, he entered in alone and cried aloud for his adversary. Forthwith there came a knight to meet him, or the semblance of a knight, armed (as it seemed) even as he was armed. With shield displayed and levelled spears they dashed together, and the horsemen reeled with the shock of their conflicting steeds; but Osbert avoided the other's lance, which slid harmlessly from him, while he for his part unhorsed his foe. But the fallen knight started from the ground; and, seeing Osbert seize the reins of his horse, that he might take it thence for a prize, he brandished his lance, hurled it like a javelin, and pierced Osbert's thigh with a grisly wound. Our knight, for his part, whether he felt no wound for joy of his victory or that he dissembled his pain, let his adversary disappear and rode away in triumph. The horse thus won he handed over to his squire—a great charger, swift and agile and most fair to see. His household crowded to welcome his return, marvelling at this event, rejoicing in the overthrow of the fallen knight, and chanting the prowess of their renowned lord. Then Osbert disarmed; and, taking off his steel chausses,[1] he found one full of clotted blood. His household were aghast at the wound, but the lord scorned all fear. Meanwhile the townsfolk rose from their beds and were gathered together; for the marvel grew from minute to minute, and dispelled all drowsiness even from those who had so lately been weighed down with sleep. The horse, pledge of this victory, was held with a free rein and shown to the public gaze; men admired his flashing eyes, his proud neck, his jet-black coat and the equal blackness of his saddle and trappings. And now the first

1. Stockings of chain mail reaching almost to the waist.

cock crowed; whereupon the horse began to bound and prance, snorting with open nostrils and pawing the ground, until he had burst his reins and galloped off in native liberty, disappearing from the eyes of those who would have pursued him. Moreover, our noble lord kept this lifelong memorial of his wound, that yearly on this same day and this same hour the ancient scar would open and bleed afresh. Wherefore, not many years afterwards, he crossed the seas [to the Holy Land], where he fought doughtily in many battles against the pagans and ended his days in the service of God.

Index